PHOTO: *Rosalind Mann*

DOROTHY PICKLES is a well-known British broadcaster and political scientist who teaches at the London School of Economics.

Democracy

IDEAS IN ACTION
General Editor: Professor Maurice Cranston

Democracy

DOROTHY PICKLES

Basic Books, Inc., Publishers, New York

© 1970 by Dorothy Pickles
Library of Congress Catalog Card Number: 79 130524
SBN: 465 01599 9

Printed in Great Britain

Contents

Part I
Conceptions of Democracy

I

What is Democracy?

It has been said that democracy is the worst form of government
except all those other forms that have been tried from time to time.

Winston Churchill in the House of Commons, 1947

... until about a hundred years ago democracy was a bad thing ...
in the next fifty years it became a good thing, and ... in the last
fifty years it has become an ambiguous thing.

C. B. Macpherson in The Real Meaning of Democracy

... democracy is more complex and more intricate than any other
political form.

Giovanni Sartori in Democratic Theory

The Changing Political Climate

One of the most difficult questions to answer satisfactorily is:
What *is* democracy? Not only is there no agreed definition, but
some definitions are so vague as to be virtually useless and others
so specific as to be obviously incomplete. Linguistically, the
word simply means government by the people. But this leaves
a great many problems unsolved. No political system at any
time, democratic or not, has ever provided for *all* the people
even to choose the government, much less to exercise governmental powers. In different times, and in different countries,
citizenship has been restricted on a number of grounds. Age,
sex, literacy, property, social status and sometimes colour and
religion, have all at one time or another barred certain people
from the enjoyment of political rights enjoyed by others. Sometimes the restrictions are logical and common-sense ones, for
instance, the denial of the vote to children and the insane on the
ground that they are incapable of taking responsible decisions.
But many restrictions have been based on prejudices which, in

the political climate of the time, were taken for granted as self-evident truths. Until almost the end of the last century, it was taken for granted everywhere that women ought not to enjoy the same political rights as men. As late as 1892, Gladstone was opposing women's suffrage on the following grounds: 'I have no fear lest the woman should encroach upon the power of the man. The fear I have is lest we should invite her unwittingly to trespass upon the delicacy, the purity, the refinement, the elevation of her own nature, which are the present sources of its power.'[1] Translated into less pompous language, this simply meant that, in Gladstone's view, politics constituted a dirty game and men must decide on behalf of women whether the latter were too pure to be involved in it! In Great Britain, women did not have full suffrage rights until 1929. French women did not obtain them until 1945. In the United States, the battle for full recognition, in practice as well as in theory, of negro citizenship on exactly the same terms as those applicable to white Americans is not yet won everywhere. In Switzerland women still do not have the vote except in some local elections. Yet Great Britain, the United States and Switzerland have long been generally recognised as democracies.

If the term 'government by the people' is taken to mean the formulation and carrying out of national policy by the whole electorate, then it has certainly never existed and is unlikely to exist in the future. It has always been interpreted in practice to mean government by some or by a few on behalf of the rest. Until recently the idea that everybody should have at least an equal opportunity to become one of the few or to share in the exercise of high executive functions was not generally acceptable. In Great Britain, Catholics, Jews and agnostics could not even become Members of Parliament until well on in the last century, and membership of governments was still at that time restricted in the main to the nobility, the gentry and the middle classes. Below them, there was, in Harold Laski's phrase, 'the mob that did not count'. The right of all to compete on equal terms for entry to the higher ranks of the Civil Service was not achieved in practice until well into the present century. And in countries whose claim to consider themselves as democracies is not seriously contested anywhere this side of the Iron Curtain, not everybody enjoys today an adequate opportunity of influencing and deciding on government policies. Certainly some have far more opportunities than others.

One difficulty in defining democracy arises from the fact that political systems are in a continual state of evolution. Things that are inconceivable in the political climate of one period of history become not merely possible in another, but so generally accepted that they are taken for granted. In every age there will be a number of blind spots, of attitudes that are accepted without question as part of the nature of things. It was taken for granted for years that British citizenship was given at the age of 21. Then this habit began to be questioned, and Britons now have the vote at the age of 18. Ideas regarding what ought to be the scope of governmental intervention in the lives of individuals have also changed and are continually changing. In the nineteenth century, democratic government was seen mainly in terms of equality of political and legal rights, of the right to vote, to express differing political opinions and to organise political opinion through political parties, of the right of elected representatives to supervise or control the activities of the government of the day. Today, much more stress is laid upon the need for the State to guarantee to everybody certain economic and social rights, involving the elimination of educational, and social inequalities.

As ideas change, so the content of the word 'democracy' changes in people's minds. In the last century, though parliamentary government had by then long been generally accepted in Great Britain, not all its supporters believed that it ought to be democratic as well as parliamentary. Disraeli, for instance, held that democracy was 'a thoroughly vicious form of government'. Today, democracy is held in such esteem all over the world, that all countries are anxious to pay lip service to it. As J. K. Galbraith put it recently, 'Like the family and truth and sunshine and Florence Nightingale, democracy stands above doubt.'[2] In 1949, a UNESCO enquiry on democracy by more than 100 scholars received not a single reply hostile to democracy. 'Probably for the first time in history (says the report), democracy is classed as the proper ideal description of all political and social organisations advocated by influential proponents.'[3]

A consequence of this change of attitude has been that the term is now used to describe so many different forms of government that there are serious risks of its becoming not merely ambiguous but totally meaningless. It serves too often less to explain how systems work than to justify some and decry others. In *The Essentials of Parliamentary Democracy*, first published in the 1930s, Reginald Bassett deplored the fact that 'people can employ the term democracy to cover anything and everything they regard as desirable; and there are even some who use it to cover anything they think undesirable.'[4] Since then, some 30 African States have joined Egypt, South Africa, Liberia and Ethiopia as independent States, all of them describing themselves as democracies. African, Asian and Caribbean countries that have become independent since the setting up of the United Nations after the war now number almost 60. Many countries, including all the Communist States, regularly deny to other countries the right to call themselves democracies. Thus Communists often describe their own systems as 'social' or 'people's' democracies, and the systems they dislike as 'bourgeois' democracies, implying, when they do not say so in so many words, that only their own systems are 'true' democracies. Most Western democracies deny that Communist systems are democratic in the sense in which they apply the term to themselves.

It is evident, then, that the term 'democracy' is used to cover a wide range of political systems, some of which are old and experienced, others relatively new and inexperienced. Their rate of advance towards their political, social and economic goals varies widely. In nineteenth-century Britain and America, there already existed stable systems of government with many essentially and other potentially democratic characteristics. A century later it is still far from certain that the existing democratic and republican system of government in France will last. In many of the new African States democratic constitutions were overthrown after only a few years and replaced, perhaps only temporarily, by some form of authoritarian or military rule. The building up of stable democratic government has been far easier in countries that do not have profound or passionate religious, racial, tribal or political differences, or that have frontiers secure from the danger of invasion, as those of the U.S.A. have been and as those of Great Britain were from 1066 to 1914. From the end of the seventeenth century onward, the British were more or less agreed both on the form of government and on the dominant religion, and so were able to avoid many bitter political disputes such as those that divided the North and the South in

America, monarchists and republicans in France and Catholics and non-Catholics in a number of European countries. The fact that the 13 States that originally constituted the United States had the same political background of British rule, the same habits of thought in relation to individual rights and the rule of law, and that they were all Protestant helped to make it possible for them to agree at the end of the eighteenth century on a Constitution that they have retained to this day with only 25 formal amendments (though there have, of course, been many more informal and unwritten adaptations).

Democracy as a System of Government

Even if the term 'democracy' is used to describe the United States system of government and those systems of Western Europe whose claims to it are recognised by each other to be valid, there is still plenty of room for divergent views and for misunderstandings of what is implied by the word. But within this framework, and in the political climate of the twentieth century, it is possible to supply something like a definition. As a minimum, democracy is a system of government, a set of institutions, that fulfils at least two essential requirements. It must, first, be able to elicit as accurately as possible the opinion of as many people as possible on who shall be their representatives and on how the country ought to be governed. This means as a minimum, universal suffrage, political parties, and the organisation of free voting in uncorrupt elections at relatively frequent intervals. Second, it must provide ways of ensuring that those chosen by the public do in fact do what the electorate wants them to do or that they can be replaced if they do not, even between elections. The fulfilment of this requirement entails methods of supervising the work of governments, of keeping them in constant contact with public opinion. In other words, the process of government in a democracy is essentially a dialogue between rulers and ruled. Dictators can achieve power by the use of regular electoral machinery, as Hitler did, but they then maintain themselves in power either by manipulating public opinion in their favour or by ignoring or repressing its free expression.

How effective the dialogue will be will depend on national habits and circumstances as well as on the kind of machinery by which the contacts are maintained. It has often been said that the French Fifth Republic was a dictatorship under General de Gaulle because he and not the government made policy, although the President is not responsible to the National Assembly. But the French constitution does provide machinery to meet the two basic requirements of the above definition. French Deputies and electors have precisely the same remedies as have British Members of Parliament and electors, if they do not like the policies applied by the government. They can turn it out and defeat the majority party in elections. For a series of reasons, for some of which General de Gaulle was not responsible, a majority of both deputies and electors repeatedly reaffirmed their support for General de Gaulle and for his policies. There was not what British and American citizens would describe as an effective dialogue, but that was because, for the time being, the majority of French citizens did not want to use the machinery in order to compel General de Gaulle to choose between submitting to their will, resigning or resorting to unconstitutional behaviour.

In order to fulfil the requirements of a democratic system modern democracies have evolved a number of complex institutions, and as States come to play more and more important roles in national life their number and complexity continually increase. Up to the middle of the last century, most of the citizen's life was the concern not of the State, but of the local or professional community in which he lived or worked, together with the landlord, the employer and the family. With the assumption by the modern State of responsibility for vast social and economic services—transport and health services, the control of working conditions, educational services, and so on—there has grown up a whole gamut of organisations on both national and local levels to supervise the working of government-controlled services, to supply and receive information on government policies and to exert pressure on government departments. Although these can help to maintain contacts and to make governments responsive to public opinion on specific issues, it has become difficult to ascertain with any accuracy what public opinion really is on complex and technical matters. Consent, as obtained through the machinery of political parties and elections, can, therefore, range from active support to passive acquiescence, in the form of a vote for the representative of a party, often in ignorance of what its leaders really stand for. To take only two examples, how is it possible to discover either by elections or by a series of referenda how the public would like the British Health Service to be organised, taking due account of the need to relate expenditure in this field to the total demands on the national budget? How could any clear opinion be elicited on such a question as that of Britain's entry into the Common Market? As far as the latter is concerned, the government itself may be obliged to take a decision in conditions in which its supporters are divided, the exact conditions of membership unclear, and the estimates by experts of the effects of membership on the national economy both contradictory and speculative? There are British citizens who either do not know what to think or do not care much one way or the other. Some are obsessed with their own sectional interests and know and care little about the possible effects on the country as a whole. Some could be persuaded by ingeniously worded questions and by propaganda to answer in a dozen or more contradictory ways any questions designed to elicit their wishes. Similar difficulties arise in almost every field in which political institutions nowadays affect the lives of citizens.

This situation has been to a large extent responsible for the present tendency, particularly among American behaviourist political scientists, to regard traditional democratic theories of consent and participation, or dialogue, as unrealistic and out-of-date. The contemporary passion for observing and measuring statistically, by opinion polls and other devices, how people behave has led them to conclude that the mass of the public prefers passive acquiescence to active consent and refuses to accept the responsibilities of participation. In his *Representative Government*, published in 1861, John Stuart Mill wrote that

> the only government which can fully satisfy all the exigencies of the social state is one in which the whole people participate, that any participation, even in the smallest public function, is useful; that the participation should everywhere be as great as the general degree of improvement of the community will allow, and that nothing less can be ultimately desirable than the admission of all to a share in the sovereign power of the state.[5]

Behaviourist political scientists can quote impressive statistics to show that less than one-third of the electorate is really interested in politics, that many of those who vote do so without giving any rational consideration to the issues, and often apparently without any serious thought at all, and that few can give clear explanations of why they vote as they do. 'Even when voters are well-informed, their knowledge reinforces inclinations more than it contributes to a free decision.'[6] Studies of voting behaviour have, therefore, led many contemporary students of politics to reject the classical assumptions about the need for citizen participation as at best inadequate and at worst idealistic and over-optimistic. As one of the best known of these theorists, Robert Dahl, puts it,

> If one regards political equality in the making of decisions as a kind of limit to be achieved, then it is axiomatic that this limit could only be arrived at with the complete participation of every adult citizen. Nevertheless, what we call democracy —that is, a system of decision-making in which the leaders are more or less responsive to the preferences of non-leaders —does seem to operate with a relatively low level of citizen participation. Hence it is inaccurate to say that one of the necessary conditions for 'democracy' is extensive citizen participation.[7]

In plain English, this simply means that, in Robert Dahl's view, most people are politically apathetic and that this fact does not necessarily invalidate the claim of States to be democracies, which is true, but totally beside the point. Mill did not say that the extent of participation that he considered desirable was likely to be obtainable. Nor do other supporters of the traditional approach. What he did say was that, wherever people are able and willing to participate in the processes of government, provision ought to be made for them to do so, because he believed that the quality of a democracy could be judged by the extent of citizen participation. To say that most people do not want to or cannot participate is merely to say that most existing democracies are far from ideal, which is hardly a world-shaking discovery. One could go farther and add, though Mill did not, that it is one of the rights of man to choose not to participate. If it is an essential requirement of democracy that the citizen has the right to make his voice heard, and that provision shall be made for it to be heard, it is not a requirement that he shall make his voice heard if he prefers to remain silent. Naturally, the more citizens refrain from participating, the poorer will be the quality of the democracy in the long run, though this tendency can be offset by the willingness of the apathetic to allow those who are interested and anxious to participate to do their thinking for them. This was, in fact, what Mill was counting on to improve the quality of democracy. But it is not and never has been 'one of the necessary conditions for democracy' that there shall be '*extensive* citizen participation', though it may be one of the conditions for *good* democracy. Only in an *ideal* democracy, unlikely to exist in reality, could complete participation be envisaged. It can therefore for all practical purposes be left out of account.

Whether or not people can be described as expressing 'rational' opinions is equally irrelevant to a consideration of the conditions for democracy. If the behaviourists can measure what people *do*, they cannot provide any more convincing evidence than anyone else of the relationship between what they do and why they do it. Not all wise decisions are necessarily rational, nor can any individual necessarily be relied on to give either rational or articulate explanations of his actions. Nor is there any objective criterion of rationality. All that can be said with reasonable certainty is that if too many citizens are apathetic or stupid, then the political system that they live under, whether democratic or not, will reflect some of their intellectual and political shortcomings. If they are citizens in a democracy, the quality of that democracy will indubitably suffer. But as long as there is provision for dialogue, or citizen participation, and as long as government rests on consent, or at least on acquiescence, the system remains a democracy of sorts, even if the dialogue is of poor quality.

Regarded solely as a system of government, however, a democracy provides merely the means of achieving whatever ends the community seeks to achieve. It must be possible for the democratic dialogue to relate the desirable and the possible and, in deciding what is to be done today, to take adequate account of what it is hoped can be done tomorrow or the day after. If the essential characteristics of a working democratic system are consent and dialogue, the essential spirit of a democracy depends on its conception of what constitutes 'the good life'.

D

Democracy as a Way of Life

The philosophical or moral approach, which sees democracy primarily, not in terms of means, that is of the actual political institutions providing the democractic machinery, but of ends, that is of the essential purposes that this machinery is intended to serve, is, of course, far older than the institutional approach. It was possible to dream about what social organisation ought ideally to be like long before it was possible to try to put these theories to the test. It is still the approach preferred by many modern citizens who are not actively interested in the processes of politics, and so are not prepared to be active members of parties, pressure groups and all the other political or professional organs through which political and economic interests and opinions are expressed and influence is exerted. They tend to see democracy in simpler terms, as 'not so much a programme, more a way of life'.

In reality, of course, both approaches are necessary if democracy is to be a progressive concept, as it must be if it is to survive. If the institutional approach is considered in isolation, it is static and purposeless. The moral approach, considered in isolation, easily becomes escapist or Utopian, because it is not possible to discover how far principles and ideas are realistic until attempts are made actually to put them into practice. When Sir Thomas More wrote his *Utopia* he was not formulating policies for any actual or conceivable government. He was imagining a situation in which men lived better lives, in a dream world. This can be a very useful thing to do, because it can stimulate men's imagination, make them more self-critical, enable them to see themselves in a fresh light unhampered by the prejudices and habits of their own environment. But the utility of the operation has its limits. Although, in theory, nothing impedes the free rein of the imagination, in practice, the human imagination is itself limited and confined within certain limits set by history and tradition, by the climate of opinion and by ideas that even dreamers and philosophers can take for granted as part of the nature of things, because it does not occur to them to think otherwise. A political philosopher who is too far out of line with his contemporaries is liable to be dismissed as an impractical dreamer, an eccentric not to be taken seriously. He may be persecuted, or compelled to deny publicly what he knows to be the truth, if he is too far ahead of his time. Joan of Arc was burned at the stake because she listened to voices not recognised as authentic by the Church to which she and all her contemporaries belonged. Galileo had publicly to deny what he knew to be the truth, namely that the earth revolved round the sun, a view rejected by everybody else at the time.

To a great extent chance determines the precise moment at which a particular audience will be receptive enough to absorb new ideas. And whether new ideas ever succeed in modifying the climate of opinion permanently will depend on how far any machinery exists or is devised to enable them to be tested by practical application. To try to define democracy wholly in terms of ideals and goals, however essential these may be as stimuli and criteria is, therefore, not very helpful.

Another disadvantage of this approach is that such definitions tend to be even vaguer and more subjective than definitions in terms of institutions. Democracy described as a society with 'liberty and justice for all', or as 'a way of life in a society in which each individual is believed to be entitled to an equality of concern as regards the chances of participating freely in the values of that society',[8] or as a society in which 'the people solemnly resolve (in the words of the preamble to the Constitution of India) to secure to all citizens

JUSTICE, social, economic and political;
LIBERTY of thought, expression, belief, faith and worship;
EQUALITY of status and opportunity;
　and to promote among them all
FRATERNITY assuring the dignity of the individual and the unity of the nation;

—these give no guidance to governments as to *how* societies can be organised to provide these things. How can phrases like 'equality of concern' or 'liberty and justice for all' be translated into acts? How can measures intended to produce equality be prevented from merely imposing uniformity, which is surely the negation of liberty? How much liberty can be permitted to individuals or groups without creating the danger that they will use these liberties to deprive other individuals and groups of their liberties? How can any society impose fraternity? People do not love each other in obedience to Acts of Parliament. General definitions of this kind—and democratic constitutions are full of them—tend to encourage cynicism unless it is possible to show what the words mean in terms of institutions. Merely as declarations of intentions, they can lead people to conclude that democracy is simply 'a high-flown name for something that does not exist',[9] or even for something that cannot exist.

What Democracy Is Not

One advantage of looking at democracy in terms of institutions, but at the same time keeping their essential purposes in mind, is that it can help us to avoid some common misunderstandings about it. One of the most widespread is that democracy is a synonym for majority rule. In the short run, democratic systems have to rely on universal suffrage and majority rule when, as usually happens, no general agreement or compromise is possible between differing conceptions of how society ought to be organised. But it is evident that majority rule can be effective only with the tacit or explicit consent of the minority. Where minorities come to believe that they are being unfairly treated or even persecuted by the majority, they will sooner or later cease to acquiesce in majority rule. In some of the new African States, for instance, governments muzzle opposition movements, by banning them, by putting their leaders in prison, or by restricting freedom of expression. In such conditions there can, in the long run, be no stable government. As soon as the opposition becomes powerful enough it will overthrow the government by *coup d'état* or revolution, as has happened already more than once in a considerable number of African States. Where an opposition is not powerful enough to challenge the majority it will go underground. The State will then be faced perpetually with the threat of disturbance, and even of anarchy or civil war, and so will perpetually be tempted to resort to repressive measures in order to forestall the danger. The mere fact that in such States there is majority rule, that 80 or 90 per cent of the electorate vote for the government, should not be allowed to obscure the fact that, unless both minority and majority views are put fairly to the electorate, an election cannot be regarded as a reliable test of opinion. What exists is a democratic façade, not the reality.

It is often argued that most of the young African States can-

not afford the luxury of opposition parties. They are still inexperienced and they have not the political, economic or administrative resources to enable them to cope at one and the
same time with all the practical and urgent problems that they
have to face, let alone with the additional problem of organising
freedom for opposition movements. This is probably so. But
what the argument amounts to is that, in such circumstances,
the conditions for effective democratic government are not present. These include the kind of responsible give and take, tolerance of minority views, opportunities for full and free discussion
that exist in Western democracies because they are the result
of a long training in self-government, which has entailed the
growth over the years of complex machinery to safeguard individual rights and freedom of opinion, and to protect the citizen
against injustice from the State. These have included organised parties, pressure groups, a free press, an uncorrupt civil
service, independent courts of law, and so on. All this requires
long experience, as well as a high level of educational and social
development. Most of the new African States are educationally,
politically and economically backward, with a high proportion
of illiterate citizens who are politically naive and cannot be expected to discriminate between the possible and the impossible,
the responsible and the irresponsible. The fact that many of
them have not yet acquired any settled national loyalties and
have to wrestle with tribal as well as political oppositions is an
additional complication.

It is thus no accident that democracy took root in societies
that were relatively wealthy and sophisticated. What has led to
the habit of describing systems as democratic even though
they differ so radically from those of Western countries that
no meaningful definition could include both is, first, the present-
day prestige of the democratic label, and, second, the fact that
these new systems do have democratic goals, and are trying to
apply *some* democratic principles, and hoping at some future
date to apply more. Most of their constitutions are, or were at
first intended to be, modelled on Western democratic constitutions. Moreover, Western democracies have their own weaknesses and imperfections. Some political theorists have, therefore, preferred to widen the definition and to regard developing
States, Communist systems and Western democracies as so
many different approaches to democratic government, each of

which has its own priorities and its own route. On this basis, the one-party rule common in young African States could claim to be democratic, on the ground that 'there is in these countries a general will, which can express itself through, and probably only through, a single party.' Communist working-class rule could be defended as democratic because 'it would comprise the great majority of the population, and because its purpose would be the humanisation of the whole people.'

This approach, adopted by C. B. Macpherson in his study *The Real World of Democracy* (from which the above quotations are taken), is defended by him on the ground that democracy can be defined in a broad or a narrow sense. In this broad sense, however, it is not a definition at all, but an acceptance at face value of the assumption of Communist and one-party States that they are entitled to call themselves democracies (and to be recognised as such) on the strength of what they hope to become, irrespective of the means by which they seek to achieve their ends, or of their chances of achieving the ends by the means chosen. But democracy is concerned with means as well as ends and majority rule is only one of the means. There are others that neither Communism nor any other one-party system believes in. One of them is that genuine democratic government must involve a genuine dialogue between different strands of opinion, and particularly between supporters and opponents or potential opponents of the system.

No doubt, most governments do honestly believe that they are acting in the general interest and intend to do so. But in Lord Acton's famous phrase: 'Power tends to corrupt and absolute power corrupts absolutely.' Which means that the more fervently they believe that they do represent the general interest, the more impatient they will be of opposition that hampers their action. And from there it is only a step to making sure that the government's view of what is in the general interest shall prevail. But the free expression of minority interests (though not necessarily in the *form* in which they demand it, if it constitutes a threat to the stability of the State) is essential to the democratic process, precisely because the criterion by which democratic States decide what is expedient and right is the verdict of public opinion. If half, or a quarter, or even a small proportion of opinion is muzzled, the picture that emerges from a consultation of the people is a distorted one. The dilemma of some new African States is precisely that even a limited degree of freedom for minorities does, in their present precarious stage of political development, often present a real danger to the State.

Of course, no democracy is perfect. But in order to function effectively as a democracy it must as a minimum provide for such a dialogue. There must, in other words, be sufficient basic agreement among citizens on how this can be done to enable minorities to believe that the methods adopted offer them a reasonable chance of one day getting their own way by constitutional means, that is, by the use of regular and accepted procedures, instead of by revolution or riot. It does not have to be a *good* chance (some minorities represent only a small fraction of opinion), or even a short-run chance. The essential condition is that there shall be a 'consensus' on the rules of the political game. It is because some Negroes in some parts of the United States have lost their belief in the efficacy of the methods that they are resorting at times and in certain places to force. The majority have up to now remained convinced that the democratic methods, whatever their inadequacies, still give them a better chance of ultimate victory than do any conceivable alternative methods.

Naturally, there must always be the risk of ultimate resort to violence by minorities. Most democracies at one time or another have to deal with outbreaks, ranging from serious disorder to sporadic riots or demonstrations. But while the State retains its authority, these need not threaten the democratic way of life. Demonstrations, strikes, or marches can be warning signs of an evolution of opinion that wise governments will take into account. In other words, no majority should exacerbate minorities beyond bearing if that can be avoided, for 'revolutions happen when evolution is too long delayed'. On the other hand, if a minority drives a majority into repressive action, then the price to be paid may be the breakdown of the whole system of democratic government. Where minorities do not enjoy the freedom to propagate their views, however, there is no justification for describing the system as democratic and, in one-party States that freedom does not exist.

In the case of Communist States, there is an additional reason for denying their right to call themselves democratic. Where developing States often refuse to provide for a democratic dialogue for reasons of expediency, Communist States object to such dialogue on principle. In their eyes, the governmental process is not a dialogue at all, but a monologue by Communist leaders who are convinced that their views are the only 'correct' ones, and that their job is to lead the public to 'recognise' them as objective truths. The Communist doctrine, as laid down by Marx and interpreted by Lenin, is regarded as having defined once and for all the right course of action. The Communist Party of the Soviet Union is the recognised body which interprets this doctrine (though the claim is now disputed by the Chinese Communist leaders who also claim to have a monopoly of political truth). The rest merely say 'yes' or 'no', or suggest minor amendments and criticisms. Attacks on Communist leaders, if they challenge policies and principles—and sometimes even if they challenge only methods—are, therefore, regarded as treason. There is a gulf between the two concepts for, as Herbert Agar has put it, 'no democrat can be certain that his economic and social philosophy is right; no Communist can imagine that his is wrong'.[10]

Another misunderstanding of the nature of democracy is to assume that political systems can do more than they actually can. Some democrats believe, for instance—as Marxists also do—that in an ideal society the concept of class would disappear, and that the creation of a classless society should, therefore, be one of the essential aims of democracies. But this is only one among many varied goals, and moreover one on which democrats are by no means agreed. If it were to be a requirement of a democracy, the title would have to be denied to all systems existing today or likely to exist in the foreseeable future. In Britain and the United States, the two oldest and most experienced democratic systems, considerable social and economic disparities still exist, nor is there anything approaching a classless society in any Communist country. The principle itself is, moreover, so vague and so susceptible of differing interpretations that it would be impossible to imagine any general agreement on how to apply it. The same is true of principles such as 'economic equality', 'equality of opportunity' and 'social injustice'. Experience suggests that such ideals must always remain to some extent unattainable, because as some inequalities are eliminated, others become perceptible and so the goal of equality, or classlessness or whatever it may be, eternally recedes. For example, the condition of a true democratic dialogue—free speech, free elections, freedom of opinion, freedom of political parties and professional associations, the right of the citizen to equality before the law and to equal opportunities for social and economic betterment—all these have been modified again and again in terms of their implementation through actual institutions, as successive generations have reinterpreted them. The process is likely to be unending, because people are perpetually changing, and a democracy must reflect these changes.

Democratic governments, moreover, have to exist in the real world, in which they are hampered by obstacles of all kinds, both human and inanimate, national and international. No political system can carry out more than a fraction of its programme at any given time. The tools with which governments have to work are clumsy, and so there are some things that States cannot be expected to do quickly and others that they ought not to be expected to do at all, because political methods alone are incapable of doing them.

One example of the difficulty of deciding what politics can and cannot do is provided by the contemporary British quarrel about how the national educational system ought to be organised. It is maintained by some that, so long as different sections of the community send their children to schools that have different 'status symbols' attached to them, it will never be possible to create a classless community, which they hold to be one of the duties of a democracy. Some opponents of their solution to this problem—the generalisation of 'comprehensive schools' —can argue that an educational system is intended primarily to educate and that the real purposes of education ought not to be subordinated to attempts to create particular social systems; that, even if it were justifiable to try to do this, political decisions relating to school systems would be ineffective, because snobbery and class distinctions are deep-rooted and caused by a number of complex factors, only some of which would be affected by educational reforms. Political decisions, for instance, cannot be guaranteed to change social, professional, psychological and family attitudes. It could also be argued that, by introducing compulsory 'comprehensive' schools, any decrease in social inequality would be obtained only at the cost of a decrease in the existing degree of liberty of parents to choose the kind of school that they want for their children. As so often happens in politics, in solving, or trying to solve, one problem, there is a risk of creating others, for there is no unanimity on the balance of advantages and disadvantages involved in replacing the present known system by a new and relatively untried one.

The Difficulties of Democratic Government

Though it is, in practice, impossible to separate ends from means, trying to keep both constantly in mind and adapted to each other helps to make democracy the most difficult and complex of all forms of government. Any example of legislation intended to increase liberty, diminish inequality, provide justice, and so on, provides a string of dilemmas far harder to resolve than the educational example just quoted. It is relatively easy to agree on the desirability of diminishing inequalities, whether political, legal, economic or social, but very difficult indeed to reach agreement on how that can or should be done, and the interpretation of what is involved in trying to apply certain principles is continually changing. Thus, in Dicey's day, equality before the law was taken to mean the right of all to be tried in the same courts on the basis of the same laws. In the middle of the twentieth century it also means the right of all to the necessary financial and legal aid to enable them to make use in practice of the rights that they enjoy in theory. Some years ago, when British government or local programmes of housing or road-building called for the compulsory acquisition of private property, the authorities were not obliged to pay full compensation, presumably on the ground that the public good ought to take precedence over private rights. Now authorities are obliged to pay the 'market value' to the owner of such property, and where no agreement can be reached on the appropriate figure there are provisions for appeals against decisions of local authorities and government departments. The principle has not changed. But the conditions of its application have come to take more account of other principles, among them that of the need not to impose more hardship than strictly necessary on the individual in order to promote the good of the community. There are still many fields, however, in which citizens feel that 'liberty and justice for all' do not yet exist and new devices to remedy inadequacies are continually being suggested. A recent innovation is the appointment in Great Britain of a Parliamentary

Commissioner, or Ombudsman, whose function is to investigate complaints made to M.P.s alleging injustice to individuals as a result of government policies.

Problems of this kind are likely to be endless, for no sooner is one solved than a new one crops up. For example, it was assumed by many British supporters of the National Health Service that it would not only do away with all serious inequalities between citizens arising from sickness, but that it would probably eventually supersede all private medical services. In fact, owing to a number of unforeseen circumstances, the system had within 20 years become so inadequate that it was threatening to collapse, owing to shortage of nurses, hospitals, equipment and also of medical personnel, some of whom were seeking to return to private practice or going abroad.

As democratic government has extended the scope of its activities, the need for more and more intermediary bodies has grown. They are needed to provide more effective contacts between the citizen and the State, and also to provide the necessary coordination between different policies at home and between the policies of different nations. At the same time, a host of organisations have become necessary simply to explain to citizens what government policies are and why they ought to be supported or opposed. And because the issues are often highly technical and difficult for laymen to understand, attempts to present them to mass audiences involve both supporters and opponents in oversimplifications and some deliberate fostering of myth and legend.

The multiplication in Western democracies of intermediary bodies can certainly help to make the democratic dialogue more effective. But it can also increase the average citizen's sense of remoteness from the modern State. The more elaborate the devices for ascertaining opinions, explaining policies, exerting pressure, the more he may feel himself a helpless cypher, condemned by his lack of knowledge and expertise to accept the judgement of others or merely to follow the lead of the party or the particular professional organisations—trade unions or interest groups—to which he belongs. Democratic States are thus confronted by perpetual dilemmas in trying to decide how far their institutions help and how far they hinder the maintenance of good relations between rulers and ruled.

Some of the differences between democratic systems arise

from their differing attempts to deal with these and other dilemmas. Some arise from differing national conditions, social, political and economic, others from differing national traditions, that is from climates of opinion created by past history and conditions. In the following chapters a number of democratic ideas and methods will be discussed, in the hope of illustrating both the variety of actual and possible approaches to democracy and the problems involved in practical attempts to put democratic principles into practice. For though democracy is largely taken for granted in America and Western Europe as the only desirable system of government, it still remains not only the most difficult system to define, but also the most difficult system to work.

2

Direct Democracy

Athens provides almost a laboratory experiment in popular government: except that it all happened so long ago, and so far away, and in a language which is so very dead, it might almost be worth our while to pay it some attention.

H. D. F. Kitto, The Greeks

The Greek experiment in democracy is generally considered to have provided important lessons for the world today, partly because it was the first known example, partly because it was carried out in circumstances that can never be repeated, and that make it possible to study a much simpler form of democratic government than would be conceivable in modern, complex, industrial societies. It has been assumed that an analysis of what could be regarded as the essential elements of democratic government may help to explain the basic conditions for success and so provide some insight into the weaknesses of modern democracies. On the other hand, it can be argued that, since the Greek experiment is so far away from us in ideas as well as in time, it is peculiarly liable to be misunderstood by modern minds and study of it may increase rather than diminish the contradictions, misconceptions and ambiguities that characterise modern democratic theories. For one thing, there were many Greek city States (not all of them democratic) and relatively little is known about how their governments actually worked. Accounts of Greek democracy usually relate only to Athenian government in the fifth and fourth centuries B.C., the system and the period about which most is known.

Much of our information even about that period is incomplete and scrappy, and often available to us only at second-hand. The much quoted contemporary description of the system by

Pericles, the greatest of the Athenian leaders, was given in a speech delivered at a time when Athens was at war with Sparta, and what has come down to us is not even the full text of the speech, but only a reported version. Moreover, Pericles was speaking at a patriotic ceremony, and so would naturally have given a somewhat idealised picture, stressing the differences between the Athenian and Spartan systems of government.

Nevertheless, even when allowance is made for all these facts, the speech is an impressive statement of what the Athenian democracy stood for,

> We are called a democracy [he said] because the city is administered not for the few, but for the majority. . . . Liberty is the principle of our public life, and in our everyday life we are not mutually suspicious or angry with our neighbour because he pleases himself, nor do we look upon him with that kind of disapproval which, though harmless, is annoying. While we do not trouble one another by interference in private affairs, we are prevented from breaking the laws by respect for them; we obey both the magistrates and the laws, especially those which are for the protection of the injured and those unwritten laws which have the support of public opinion.[1]

Socrates, Plato and Aristotle were all, in differing ways and degress, critics of Athenian democracy, though the opinions of Socrates are known to us only through the writings of others, and particularly of Plato, and those of Aristotle have been subject to considerable rearrangement and editing by later thinkers. But the criticism of both Plato and Aristotle refer to a period when what are generally regarded as the great years of Athenian democracy were already over. When Socrates was tried and convicted in 399 B.C. Plato was 30 years old, though his Academy was not founded until some 10 years or so later. Aristotle was born 15 years later and was not an Athenian. Both lived through the years of the decline of the city State and Aristotle lived to see the final absorption of Athens in the Macedonian Empire.

What Greek Democracy Was Not

Perhaps the greatest difficulty in looking back at Greek democracy is to avoid putting it into a context of modern ideas and preconceptions that would have been totally alien to Greek thought and ways of life. The Greek system was not, for instance, national government in the modern sense of the term, but city government, though that description too is open to misunderstanding. The Greek city States are not really comparable either with modern nations or with modern cities. They were States, in the sense that they had their own independent governments and constitutions, and were not subject to some higher power, as modern city governments are subject to the control and supervision of national governments. They were cities in the sense that their areas and populations were no larger than those of modern cities. Athens is thought to have had a population of about 300,000—say, three quarters of that of Bristol in 1968 or half of that of Columbus, Ohio.

Greek government, then, was local or municipal in character as well as national. The links between citizens were much closer than those between citizens in a modern State. They were relatives, friends and neighbours, sharing a common life, a common language and a common religion, able to meet and discuss the city's affairs in the marketplace. For the most part, they spent their lives in the city, since neither modern possibilities nor habits of travel existed. Where the modern citizen has a hierarchy of loyalties—to his village or town, his county, and to England, Scotland or Wales, and, in the United States, to his village or town, his State and the Union—in fifth-century Greece, the citizen's exclusive loyalty was to the city State. 'The city', said Ernest Barker, 'was not only a unit of government; it was also a club'.[2]

The city differed from a modern city also in that it was both urban and rural. About half the Athenians lived in what today would be called a town, together with a port some four miles away. The other half lived in the country.

Another vital difference between Greek and modern society was what it is fashionable nowadays to call 'the class structure'. In modern democracies, or almost all of them, all residents born in the country or naturalised enjoy the rights of citizenship. Whatever may be said about economic and social inequalities, political and legal equality are now both recognised as a right of all citizens. And States have set up complicated machinery to ensure that economic inequality does not prevent the right to legal equality from being effectively exercised in practice. In classical Greece, residence was not a recognised qualification for citizenship. This was a hereditary right, limited to the sons of Athenians. Thus, out of a population of between 300,000 and 400,000 only 20,000 to 40,000 men were citizens,[3] a figure that will not appear very democratic to modern ways of thinking.

It must be remembered, however, not only that feminine inequality and slavery were at that time universal institutions, taken for granted, but also that citizenship was something more responsible than merely having the right to vote. It implied the right to some share in the actual government of the city, and as a minimum the right to attend the town meeting. Children, women, resident aliens (even if they had lived in the city for generations), freed slaves and slaves were all excluded from citizenship. But it would not be accurate to picture Athenian citizens as constituting a wealthy and privileged minority, a leisured class, able to concentrate their time and attention on politics and political and philosophical discussion only because hordes of oppressed slaves were working to support them. Only between a quarter and a third of the population owned slaves, and most of them probably had no more than one. The great majority of those who participated in Athenian government were, in the words of Socrates, as quoted by Xenophon, 'fullers, shoemakers, carpenters, smiths, peasants, merchants and shopkeepers'.[4] In fourth century Athens, when the city was much poorer than during the preceding century, except for a small group of relatively very rich men at the top of the social scale and a larger group of casual labourers at the bottom, wealth was fairly evenly distributed.[5]

Nor were slaves on the whole badly treated. The State did exploit some, who were employed in mines in very bad conditions. Some very wealthy citizens employed many slaves in domestic service, and some acquired wealth by hiring out slaves in skilled occupations. But slaves seem to have mixed freely with the rest of the population, and many earned good money as skilled workers. Indeed, Plato criticised the fact that the freemen and slaves were often indistinguishable in Athens. In other words, though there was political discrimination, and only citizens were as a rule allowed to own land, there was neither social segregation nor any hard and fast social distinction. Many Athenian citizens did not own any land, and, in the fourth century, over half of the citizens, then estimated at 21,000,

earned their living on very small holdings of land or as crafts-
men or shopkeepers.

Plato and Aristotle certainly believed that leisure was *ideally*
a condition of political life. But in the *real* Greek world most
citizens worked hard. Many could not afford to take time off to
carry out their political obligations, and others could do so only
thanks to the existence of a regular system of payments by the
State to compensate them, at least partially, for loss of working
time. Such payments contrast favourably with the situation in
Great Britain at the beginning of the present century. For it
was not until 1911 that M.P.s were paid salaries.

Another important difference between Athenian and modern
democracies is that they reflect radically different approaches to
politics. Modern democracy starts from the individual, for whom
politics is only one aspect of life. There is nothing sacrosanct
about the modern democratic State. The mechanisms of democratic government—its constitutions, laws, courts, police, political
parties and elections—are the means of discovering and enforcing the minimum terms on which individuals who disagree,
and who, it is assumed, will always disagree in their desires and
aims, can agree to live their private lives peaceably in the same
community. Greek democracy started from the State and saw
the individual's wellbeing as inseparable from that of the collective personality. What distinguished a democratic from an
undemocratic State was the nature of the governmental process. In a democracy, as Pericles put it, 'the administration is in
the hands of the many and not of the few'. This meant that the
whole emphasis of politics was on what men had in common—
their city life, its defence, art, religion, festivals and laws. It
was a shared way of life assumed to be the concern of all, and
so to be the responsibility of all. Where 'the many', that is a
sample or cross-section of the whole citizen body, undertook
responsibility for making and enforcing the laws, the citizen
regarded himself as being protected against arbitrary rule in
the interests of a minority. Where laws were made by the few
or by one, that is, in an oligarchy or a tyranny, the citizen had
no such guarantee. Once there, the law became a common
bond, and though the community could change it, there was a
general presumption that it was, in Ernest Barker's words,
'something given and permanent, which it was better not to
change'.[6] In other words, the Greeks fitted the individual into a

c

framework already there and the existing State was thought of as providing the right, or the best, way of life. The concept was essentially static. In modern democracy, men tailor the State to fit their own views of what is right and best and they assume that these views will continually differ and continually change. The organisation of the State will, therefore, also have to change in order to adapt to changes in public opinion. The modern concept, in other words, is essentially dynamic.

This democratic individualism is, however, a very recent development. Throughout most of the history of political thought, human diversity was generally regarded as undesirable. Its existence has been treated at some periods as being due to human wickedness, at others to imperfect institutions. It is a modern idea to regard diversity as not only normal and right but inevitable, and to regard institutions as being required to provide for its free expression.

How 'Direct Democracy' Worked

The expression 'direct democracy' is itself liable to give rise to misconceptions. The fact that the essential characteristic of the Athenian system was the equal right of all citizens to participate in the processes of government did not mean that every decision was taken at a kind of mass meeting, attended by some 20,000 or more citizens. It meant that all citizens had equal right to membership of a number of governing bodies, but these had necessarily to be of a manageable size. There were three main organs of government—the assembly of citizens, the council and the courts. The assembly held 10 sessions a year, involving some 40 meetings, and could be summoned to special meetings if necessary, for instance, in case of an emergency, or to debate particularly important issues. Its function was to discuss and decide questions of both internal and foreign policy, including defence and finance, and also to supervise the administration—the 'magistrates' who actually carried out the policies. The assembly was the sovereign body, representing the will of the people, as Parliament does in the British system. As far as is known, it was usually attended by between 3,000 and 6,000 of the citizens. The only actually recorded attendance known to us was 3,616, but it is known that a quorum of 6,000 was required for some decisions of particular importance. All citizens, that is male Athenians over 30, were free to attend and to speak, though in practice skilled orators came to exercise a predominant role, and even to constitute almost a class of 'professional' politicians. Contemporary accounts of the composition of the assembly vary a good deal, some describing it as consisting mainly of working-class members, others speaking of it as being predominantly middle-class. Plato, for instance, gives the following description of discussion in the assembly: '. . . when the debate is on the general government of the city, anyone gets up and advises them, whether he be a carpenter or a smith or a leather worker, a merchant or a sea-captain, rich or poor, noble or humble'.[7] On the other hand, he speaks of members booing and shouting down others who gave advice on technical matters such as shipbuilding, if they were not experts on the subject.

The assembly was not free, however, to decide its own agenda. The council was an executive, or steering committee, drawing up the assembly's agenda, organising and coordinating its work, and also supervising the administrative work carried out by the 'magistrates', most of whom carried out the routine administrative functions of a civil service. The council consisted of 500 members, chosen annually by lot from a panel of citizens elected by the 'demes' of Athens in proportion to their size. (Demes were electoral districts, something like urban polling districts in Great Britain, and precincts in the U.S.A.[8]). Members of the council had to be over 30 and were not allowed to serve for more than two years. The council sat every day (except for public holidays) though not in plenary session. The day-to-day work was carried out by a system of rotation, 50 members from a single tribe acting for a tenth of the year. The president was chosen by lot and could hold office for only one day in his life.

The assembly, then, decided only those issues framed by and put to it by the council. Since the latter body represented a fair cross-section of the population, it could be assumed that the views of the two bodies would not be seriously in conflict.

The third body, the 'juries', consisted of 6,000 citizens chosen annually by lot to form popular law courts. There were no professional judges or lawyers. The juries acted as guardians of the constitution and of law and order generally, and tried cases of individual misconduct as well as political crimes such as treason. The number sitting on any particular case (chosen by lot from the 6,000) varied from several hundreds to thousands in an important political case. The trial of Socrates, for instance, took place before a court of 501, of whom 281 found him guilty. The proportion of middle- to poorer-class jurors seems to have varied at different periods, the general tendency being towards the predominance of members of the middle classes.

In addition to these organs of government, 10 generals were chosen by the whole people. They commanded the army and the fleet, and controlled defence and foreign policy in general, but held no civilian office. Some of them, however, had great influence over the assembly and were listened to as political advisers. Since they were re-eligible it was possible for some to continue to hold office for a number of years and so to become real political leaders. The most famous of them, Pericles, held office for 15 years, and virtually dominated the rest. But it would be a mistake to think of them as being political leaders in the modern sense. Ernest Barker's description of them as forming 'something like a Cabinet' is liable to be misleading. For, unlike a Cabinet, they had neither direct nor collective responsibility, except as military leaders. They had no 'mandate', no common policy or corporate sense, no system of rival policies such as is provided by the modern Cabinet, Shadow Cabinet and the party system. But it must also be remembered that there was in Athenian democracy no conception of government and opposition and no hard and fast distinction between the civilian and the military aspects of government. Athenian defence was by a citizen army. In case of war, the citizen transformed himself into a soldier quite simply, by 'going home for his shield, his spear and his rations, and reporting for orders'.[9]

Is Athenian Democracy Relevant to the Modern World?

Can this system have any relevance to the problems of democracy in the modern world? Within the limits already discussed, it could certainly claim to be a real democracy. It did provide political equality in the sense that all citizens had the same political rights and the same obligations to carry out political duties and to hold public office. And these were not merely theoretical rights; they were effective in practice owing to the system of State payments to those who could not afford otherwise to accept the responsibilities. No political office was barred on grounds of wealth, status or property (though this was not true of conditions in the army, owing to the requirement that the soldier had to find his own equipment). Pericles was proud of this political equality, pointing out that 'in public esteem, when a man is distinguished in any way, he is more highly honoured in public life, not as a matter of privilege, but in recognition of merit; on the other hand, anyone who can benefit the city is not debarred by poverty or by the obscurity of his position.'[10] This did not mean, however, that Athens was a socially egalitarian society. The Athenian people were, indeed, rather snobbish in their choice of leaders. They not only made derogatory comments on politicians of humble origins, but tended to choose comparatively rich and well-born citizens for prominent diplomatic and financial offices. More humble citizens were also themselves frequently unwilling to serve in these posts. These are facts which might perhaps indicate to some of our more passionate believers in the duty of the State to use institutions in order to impose certain social attitudes that, where men either do not feel or want to be made to feel equal, they can always successfully circumvent political rules and regulations. It is possible that snobbery and class-consciousness, which are older and deeper instincts than the egalitarianism associated with modern concepts of democracy, may prove more stubborn and more complex human reactions than social reformers would like to believe them to be.

In one way, Athenian democratic methods seem peculiarly alien to twentieth-century habits. The citizen's choice of office-holders (except for generals) was made, not by weighing up the qualities desired in those who were to be chosen, but by lot. This method was probably adopted in order to prevent intrigues and 'cooked' elections. It did, no doubt, provide a fairly representative cross-section of the population. It certainly gave everybody an equal chance of being chosen for office. In the eighteenth century, Jean-Jacques Rousseau thought election by lot 'the most democratic' for this reason. Its disadvantages, however, would rule it out in the modern world. If modern civil servants were chosen by lot, then everybody would have a strictly equal chance of being chosen, but no account could be taken of the suitability or competence of those chosen to do the jobs that they were chosen for. Socrates and Plato did indeed, criticise the Athenian system on precisely these grounds. Socrates, for instance, thought it silly that the rulers of the city should be chosen by lot when 'no-one would be willing to employ a pilot or a carpenter or a flautist chosen by lot'.[11]

Two arguments can be put forward in defence of the Athenian system. The first is that it was not 'the rulers'—that is, the members of the assembly—who were chosen by lot. The 500 members of the council were so chosen, it is true, but they did not decide issues, and they were chosen not haphazardly, but from a panel of elected citizens. Choice by lot was also used for magistrates and jurors. But the functions of magistrates were relatively subordinate; they were required to provide some formal evidence of qualifications, and they were also subject to control by members of the assembly, and even liable to be dismissed for abuse of authority. Jurors are still chosen today more or less haphazardly from a large panel of ordinary citizens, on the ground that we know of no better way of determining in a court of law where truth lies than to submit the evidence to the judgment of a cross-section of ordinary public opinion. The second argument is that such a system is workable enough where the jobs in themselves do not call for any special expertise. The assumptions of the Greek city State were that life was simple enough, and problems general enough for the average citizen to be able to deal with them by the use of ordinary common sense. At least in the heydey of Athenian democracy there was perhaps enough truth in this assumption to justify the method.

The system of rotation in office can be defended and criticised on similiar grounds. In ancient Greece, politics was not a professional career, but a part-time and amateur responsibility. As far as is known, of the whole citizen body, only about a sixth (perhaps some 7,000) were actively engaged in governing at any one time. The system of rotation in office ensured that members of the council were not overburdened and that a high proportion of citizens acquired some experience of government. On the other hand, it meant that there could be no real continuity or coherent policies. This was not the disaster that it would have been in a modern industrial and welfare State. The functions of Athenian democracy were not to provide national economic plans, universal social security, or an unending 'march of progress', but to deal with the relatively few and simple problems affecting a comparatively homogeneous and stable society, forming a small closely knit community in which something like a 'general will' could reasonably be assumed to exist. Even in such a society, good government required that a sufficient number of citizens should care sufficiently about the public good to be willing to take on the responsibilities of governing. Among the factors that led to the eventual failure of this unique Greek experiment, one was precisely the growing tendency of citizens to be more interested in their private affairs than in those of the State. Those who were involved in politics became increasingly liable to form factions, to indulge in intrigues and to develop to some extent into professional politicians. Another factor was the inability of the amateur Athenian army to defend the country adequately against technically superior professional forces and military tactics. This led to the defeat of Athens by oligarchic Sparta.

Thus, even in the relatively simple conditions that existed in fifth and fourth century Athens, it was impossible to avoid two of the basic problems that face all modern industrial democracies, and that also render the transition from colonialism to independence infinitely difficult in the more backward countries. These are, first, how to decide what is the proper place of the expert in a democratic society and, second, how to ensure adequate public control of experts to satisfy the requirements of democracy without sacrificing efficiency to the search for democracy. Nowadays the citizen demands infinitely more of the State than did the Athenian citizen, and the State is far, far larger. A vast army of technicians and experts is, therefore, needed to carry out State policies. In the poor and backward ex-colonial territories there are simply not enough experts to ensure the survival of the State as an independent political entity, let alone to provide efficient government. In the richer countries the traditional framework of democratic government is becoming less and less adapted to keeping up with the rapid changes of the modern technological age, and it is becoming more difficult for politicians to keep track of what their officials are doing. We certainly cannot go back to the rule of the amateur that characterised the Athenian system. It has yet to be proved that we can adapt democratic methods to this new situation and that democracy will not be superseded by some form of technocracy, or government by experts. Most convinced democrats believe that new democratic techniques can be evolved, provided a sufficient number of citizens retain both their interest in politics and its problems, and a sense of their own responsibility for the kind of society that is being created.

The fact that Greek democracy remained an isolated experiment for some 2,000 years is, nevertheless, a salutory reminder that no political system is immune from the danger of decay. Its greatest positive contribution to today's problems is not so much its institutions as the free discussion about them by Greek politicians and philosophers. To realise how important this has been it is necessary to remember not only the differences that separate the Greek from the modern world, but also those that separated Greek democracies from surrounding States. Seen from the twentieth-century democratic viewpoint, much of Greek thought must necessarily seem remote and inapplicable, or open to criticism. Seen in its own context, Greek democracy constituted so many islands of freedom in a surrounding world dominated by oligarchical or tyrannical forms of government. Athens' nearest neighbour and eventual conqueror, Sparta, for instance, had an unbroken tradition of authoritarian rule. Though the Athenian citizen felt himself to be, far more than the modern citizen, a part of the State and subordinate to it, he felt far freer as an individual than most of the rest of the ancient world. And he saw the State essentially as the source of this freedom and its guarantor.

In particular, Athenians were proud of their freedom to discuss and criticise their system of government. Some opponents of the system were precisely critical of this freedom. Plato, for instance, noted that 'the city is full of liberty and free speech and everyone in it is allowed to do what he likes.'[12] What the modern world owes to that freedom is the beginning of the great debate about what ought to be the relations between governments and the governed, a debate that formed the basis of the whole body of European political thought. Never before or since the period of the Greek city State has there been so much concentrated high-level argument about the principles of government. For centuries, all those seriously interested in the fundamental problems of politics have found in Greek thought the kind of intellectual stimulus that Socrates claimed to be supplying to his fellow-citizens in Athens.

I am [he said] during his trial, the gadfly that God has attached to this city, and all day long and in all places I am fastening upon you and reproaching you. You would not readily find another like me. ... If you rashly put me to death, then you will remain asleep for the rest of your lives unless God in his care send you another gadfly.[13]

Though Socrates was convicted, there have been other 'gadflies' thoughout the history of political thought. Though Greek democracy disappeared, Greek thought survived and, consciously or unconsciously, directly or indirectly, all of us in Europe and in America have been influenced by it, by the critics of Greek democracy as well as by its defenders. And though the great defender of Greek democracy, Pericles, may not have given a strictly accurate picture of how it worked in practice, his words did, and still do, convey the sense of a living ideal that, making due allowance for changed circumstances, is still that of democracy today.

3

Representative Democracy

Democracy differs from all other forms of government in that it
postulates the free organization of opposing opinions.
R. M. MacIver, The Web of Government

The meaning of representative government is that the whole people
or some numerous portion of them exercise through deputies
periodically elected by themselves the ultimate controlling power.
John Stuart Mill, Representative Government

The Development of Representative Government

Some degree of representation is inherent in all political systems.
In all countries there is normally a large majority of citizens
whose political interests are limited to an intermittently active
concern with particular aspects of public policy, in so far as
these affect or may affect their individual lives. For the rest,
they are prepared to go through life accepting the political leadership of others without question. The few, that is, represent
the many. Rulers, too, whether autocratic or democratic, if they
want to survive, must maintain some contact with the ruled,
and this involves some organised form of consultation with
spokesmen who can be regarded as qualified to represent their
countrymen's views. Even authoritarian or absolute rulers, however much they may reject representative institutions on the
ground that they themselves speak for the whole people, are,
in practice, obliged to take some account of what their subjects
do and do not want, if only to enable them to recognise the
limits beyond which they risk having a revolution on their hands.
Representation is not, then, in itself a guarantee of democracy
and may, indeed, be neither elective nor democratic.

In all but the simplest of economies, the Greek system of
representation by shifting cross-sections of the population would

be prohibitively wasteful. It would also be technically impossible, except in small and homogeneous communities of the size of small towns. The Greeks themselves eventually found it unworkable because of the political apathy of much of the population. But the modern principle of representative government was slow to develop. In mediaeval Europe, monarchy was held to be a divinely ordained institution, and kings, therefore, held themselves accountable to God. They were expected, nevertheless, to respect certain rules and traditions in accordance with assumed 'natural laws' binding alike on ruler and ruled. The Church as the spiritual ruler had the right to lay down the general principles that ought to govern the Christian monarch's exercise of power. From a very early period, there were conflicts between spiritual and temporal powers regarding the boundaries of their respective spheres of sovereignty. Monarchs sometimes yielded when faced by threats of excommunication, but by no means always. By the seventeenth century, territorial monarchs were in most cases strong enough to defy the spiritual power, or at least to negotiate acceptable agreements.

With the division of Christendom from the sixteenth century onwards, most of Europe went through a long period during which the struggle for power between opposing religious sects led to assertions of the right of subjects to resist what they regarded as religious oppression by governments, and to counterclaims by monarchs that they ruled by divine right, and so could demand absolute obedience.

In England, the belief that the monarch ruled by divine right was successfully challenged in the second half of the seventeenth century, thus opening the way to claims that kings and their governments represented the people only on terms agreed to by the people themselves. As far back as the thirteenth century, knights of the shires and burgesses of boroughs were already being consulted from time to time by kings. But the time and the nature of the consultations were decided by the sovereign and not by them. Moreover, representatives summoned to give their views spoke, not for their local populations considered as so many individuals, but for collective interests, either local or professional. The representatives included only influential citizens such as property owners, hereditary peers or spokesmen for trading corporations. Their aim was to limit the exercise of royal power by establishing certain rules by which the sovereign would agree to be bound. In no sense were they putting forward anything like a national policy.

By the end of the seventeenth century, however, the authority of the English Parliament was already binding upon the monarch in a number of fields. In France, the early representative body, the States-General, had never become the recognised spokesman for the nation as a whole, and had been unable for a number of reasons to exert the kind of pressure on the king that British Parliaments came to exercise in the seventeenth century, and so an absolute monarchy was able to persist throughout the seventeenth and most of the eighteenth century, while England was developing a settled system of representative parliamentary government.

British Parliaments, though strong, were still elected, up to the nineteenth century, by only a small fraction of the population. But M.P.s were not really responsible to their electors. The democratisation of the parliamentary system came only slowly. From the seventeenth century onwards, ideas of equality and accountability cropped up from time to time in the writings of political thinkers or in a few political movements. But such views were held by only small and untypical minorities. For instance, the Diggers, a small seventeenth-century body of agrarian reformers, preached a kind of Utopian communism based on the belief that property was the root of all evil. The Levellers, a radical movement originating in Cromwell's army, believed that privilege was the root of all evil, and that all citizens should have political equality based on universal suffrage and a written constitution. They did not accept modern ideas of economic equality and a classless society, but merely rejected political privilege based on birth or on professional monopolies. They had no quarrel with the right to own property or with the existence of social distinctions. But they believed that, as citizens, all men had the right to be treated as equals.

I think [wrote the most quoted of them] that the poorest he that is in England hath a life to live as the greatest he; and therefore truly, Sir, I think it's clear, that every man that is to live under a government ought first by his own consent to put himself under that government; and I do think that the poorest man in England is not at all bound in a strict sense to that government that he hath not had a voice to put himself under.[1]

This was essentially the claim that men had the right to be represented as individuals rather than as corporations and vested interests. Such ideas were rare at the time, and both these movements were small and short-lived. In Great Britain, France and Holland, the place of the individual in the State was seen by many political thinkers in the seventeenth and eighteenth centuries within the framework of social-contract theories of government, according to which an understanding between ruler and ruled was assumed to be inherent in the nature of civilised society. This so-called 'contract' implied the willingness of citizens of a country to give up some of their 'natural' rights in return for a system of government and law that safeguarded fundamental rights, such as life, liberty and property.

The main difficulty in accepting such contractual theories (apart from the fact that nobody has demonstrated convincingly that they have ever been, or could be, applied) is that none of them provided for any agreed method of deciding when the contract had been broken. Supporters of the doctrine felt themselves free to interpret the terms of the contract to suit themselves and invoked it to justify both subservience to rulers and rebellion against them. In the sixteenth and seventeenth centuries, Protestants used contract theories to justify defiance of Catholic rulers and so helped to lead the way to theories of individual liberty. In 1651, the political philosopher, Thomas Hobbes, in his *Leviathan*, held that individuals had an equal right to choose their ruler. But once chosen, the ruler, whether monarch or assembly, must alone have the right to think and act for the community in matters of public concern. He believed that this was necessary because of the nature of man. Without a sovereign with the authority to govern on their behalf, men would, he argued, never agree and would, therefore, end by destroying society. John Locke, who wrote towards the end of the century, believed, on the contrary, that men were naturally peaceable and sociable, and that the exercise of power by rulers ought to be limited by conditions imposed by those who delegated the power. Certain of these conditions seemed to him to be laid down in 'the laws of God and of nature', as for instance, acceptance by the ruler of the principle of equality before the law, of the obligation to protect property and also to obtain consent to taxation. Since all power was, thus, in the nature of a trust granted for the purpose of obtaining a specific end, it followed that 'whenever that end is manifestly neglected or opposed, the trust must necessarily be forfeited, and the power devolve into the hands of those that gave it, who may place it anew where they shall think best for their safety and security'.[2] In 1689, the Convention declaring the English throne vacant accused James II of 'breaking the original contract between King and people'.

Contract theory as interpreted by Locke could have led England far along the road to responsible representative government, if adequate political machinery had existed to enable rights and obligations to be safeguarded in practice. Locke was not primarily interested in this aspect of the problem, but rather with the philosophical question of the nature of society. In the seventeenth century, and indeed for long afterwards, no such political machinery existed. It developed only when there was general recognition of the truth that an 'end' could be 'manifestly neglected' only if complainants had opportunities to make their own views manifest. This was not possible while the vast majority of ordinary men and women, as well as the political leaders, believed that only certain classes ought to have the right to express their views directly. In the eighteenth century these people were defined by Edmund Burke as being 'those of adult age, not declining in life, of tolerable leisure for such discussions, and of some information, more or less, and who are above menial dependence (or what virtually is such)'.[3] He estimated that such people would amount in England to about 400,000.

The decisive events heralding the change from views such as these to the attitudes characteristic of modern representative democracy were the American War of Independence and the French Revolution, which led to the first written constitutions providing for a system of government based on the acknowledged principle of the sovereignty of the people. The Declaration of Independence of 1776 states

> ... that all men are created equal; that they are endowed by their Creator with certain inalienable rights ... that to secure these rights, governments are instituted among men,

drawing their just powers from the governed; that, whenever any form of government becomes destructive of these ends, it is the right of the people to alter or abolish it, and to institute a new government, laying its foundations on such principles and organising its powers in such form, as to them shall seem most likely to effect their safety and happiness ...

The French Declaration of the Rights of Man and of the Citizen states that

Men are born free and equal in rights ... Law is the expression of the general will ... Sovereignty resides exclusively in the nation ... The nation has the imprescriptible right to change its Constitution.

During the following century and a half France was to resort frequently to the last-mentioned right and the United States as well as France and Great Britain had still a long way to go before they could justifiably claim that their representative democracies gave full expression to these principles of individual equality. Even in 1832, the passing of the first Reform Act increased the British electorate only from just over 500,000 to just over 750,000 out of a total population of some 24 millions. Dissatisfaction with its results led the Radical Chartist movement to demand in 1838, among other things, manhood suffrage, payments for M.P.s, annual elections and a secret ballot, claims that the majority of their contemporaries regarded as dangerously revolutionary. Even the Utilitarian reformers, who believed in representative government, were sceptical regarding the consequences of giving everybody the right to vote, and it was only after a prolonged struggle that full universal suffrage was finally attained in 1929, with the granting of the vote to women on the same terms as men.

In France, acceptance of the theory of popular sovereignty preceded the establishment of the representative institutions needed to put the theories into practice. Though the absolute monarchy was overthrown by revolution and a National Assembly elected in 1789, in no election during the revolutionary period were the representatives chosen by anything like the whole body of citizens. A distinction was made between active and passive citizens. Active citizens were those who were allowed to vote because they paid a certain sum in direct taxes and were not '*en état de domesticité*', or what Burke described as 'menial dependence'. Passive citizens, though not accorded the right to vote, had a right to personal protection, property and liberty. Even active citizens did not choose their political representatives directly. They merely chose a number of electors, whose qualifications were similarly restricted, and these chose the Deputies. Thus, in 1790, out of a population of some 21 millions, only $4\frac{1}{2}$ millions counted as active citizens. In Paris, 77,371 citizens chose 779 electors, who elected 24 Deputies. Although universal (male) suffrage was included in the Constitution of 1848, various devices were employed in elections between 1850 and 1870 to restrict the franchise in practice. The Third Republic saw the general acceptance, not merely of votes for all men, but also of the freedom of electors from governmental pressures, but there was little serious support for the extension of the franchise to women, who ultimately obtained the vote only in 1945.

The evolution of representative government in the United States was more rapid in some States than in others. The American constitution came into force in 1789. Power was divided between the Federal Government and the 13 constituent States, but qualifications for voting were among the matters originally left to the States. The Senate, for instance, was chosen indirectly by the State legislatures, until the Seventeenth Amendment introduced election by the people in 1913. The President, too, was to be indirectly elected. The voters merely chose an electoral college, whose function was to elect the President, the intention being that wisdom and reflection rather than popular passion should inspire their choice. In practice, these electors soon ceased to have any real say, except to ratify the popular choice of each State. The House of Representatives was from the start popularly elected, but at first electors were required to have property qualifications, though these could vary from one State to another. By the middle of the nineteenth century, adult male suffrage had become the general rule, and in 1870, the Fifteenth Amendment to the constitution extended voting rights to Negroes. Indeed, the amendment went further and forbade any restriction of voting rights 'on account of race, colour or previous condition of servitude'.

Since the constituent States remained responsible for the legislation applying these principles, it was possible for a number of them to disfranchise Negroes in practice by making registration difficult for them or by imposing electoral qualifications, such as educational or tax-paying requirements, ostensibly applying to everybody, but unlikely to be possessed by the bulk of the Negro populations, particularly in the Southern States. There were also disparities between the States regarding women's suffrage. Wyoming, for instance, allowed women to vote in 1869, but it was not until 1919 that the Nineteenth Amendment compelled States to introduce votes for women on the same terms as men. And hindrances to the exercise of the Negro vote remained common practice right up to modern times.

Parties and Representative Government

Even when all citizens have the right to elect representatives to legislative assemblies this is not enough in itself to ensure that representative government is also democratic. The member must also recognise his obligations to his constituents. Throughout the seventeenth and eighteenth centuries, British Members of Parliament not only continued to be elected by restricted and largely unrepresentative electorates, but also to be subservient to the interests of a patron who had secured their election, rather than to those of their constituents. They were inevitably torn between their obligations to represent the local interests of their constituency and the general interests of the nation. Edmund Burke saw the function of the elected representative as being to act primarily in the national interest. In his letter of 1774 to the Sheriffs of Bristol, he wrote:

> Your representative owes you not his interest only, but his judgment; and he betrays, instead of serving you, if he sacrifices it to your opinion . . . .
> Parliament is not a congress of ambassadors from different hostile interests . . . but . . . a deliberative assembly of one nation, with one interest, that of the whole . . . . You choose a member indeed; but when you have chosen him, he is not a member of Bristol, but he is a member of parliament.[4]

This meant that an election, though it decided *who* should govern, or rather who should control the government, did not decide *how*. Today, members can still constitute themselves spokesmen for particular interests of their constituencies. But they do so in circumstances that have to a great extent eliminated the conflict between local and national interests, and that have given individuals a far greater say, not only in the choice of their member, but also in the formation of the policy that he is elected to promote. The most vital change in the representative system after Burke's day was the gradual extension of the franchise to the whole adult population. As the number of voters increased, it became essential to organise support for rival candidates, and this led to the growth of national parties with a network of local branches, and with a coherent national policy to present to the electors. Another vital change, which has become much more marked in the present century, was the tremendous expansion in the social and economic functions of the State, entailing first the reorganisation of local authorities and their virtual subordination to central-government departments, and then the taking over of a number of functions and services directly by the State. These changes made government policies of much more direct and compelling interest to the average citizen.

The result of this evolution is that the present-day member of a legislative assembly no longer represents primarily either his constituency or the general interests of his nation. He represents one of two or more general programmes to which both he and the majority of his electors are in principle equally committed. In Great Britain, he is free to vote for local and sectional constituency interests only to the extent that these are compatible with the programme, or to the extent that his party permits him to take a somewhat independent line. What thinking he does on behalf of his constituents is, therefore, restricted to non-party issues, or to matters that crop up between elections and on which his party has no mandate, or to question on which he feels that he can afford to take an independent line without jeopardising his relations with his party, on whose approval he depends in order to be re-elected. For the most part, the shared loyalty to the same party that binds together the member and the majority of the constituents can override purely local or sectional interests.

The strength of parties, and their number, are both relevant in determining the closeness of the bonds between representative and party. Both in the United States and Great Britain there exist only two dominant parties, though each includes a considerable range of differing and sometimes divergent opinions. In spite of the existence of smaller formations, some more ephemeral than others, there exists in both countries a two-party system, in the sense that only the two dominant parties are ever serious contenders for power. The fact that in both countries there is a wide area of agreement between the two rival parties on the constitutional and political framework helps to restrict the area of conflict and so focuses attention more easily on concrete questions of governmental policy. In France, on the other hand, together with all other Western-type democracies, multi-party systems developed, so that the contenders for power have been coalitions of parties. Sometimes such coalitions can be as stable as a two-party system. In Sweden, coalition with the Agrarian Party helped to keep the Socialists in power for over a quarter of a century. Holland has had long periods of stable governments. But where, as has often happened in France, the members of coalitions have been scarcely less divided among themselves than from rival coalitions, then there has been, at best, weak government, since policy divisions have been blurred and party discipline weakened by frequent movement from one group to another. At worst, there have been crises leading to the downfall of the system. In Italy, in pre-Hitler Germany, in pre-war Czechoslovakia and in Belgium, too, both the number of parties and the divisions between some of them have sometimes rendered stable democratic government difficult, and even impossible.

In France, the difficulties have gone deeper and lasted longer than in most other European countries. Oscillations between republican, monarchic, imperial and dictatorial rule continued for almost a century following the Revolution. In the last quarter of the nineteenth century after the coming of the Third Republic, a settled system of republican parliamentary democracy seemed finally to have been achieved. But this régime ended in 1940 with France's military defeat and occupation by Germany. Its successor was also troubled by profound party disagreements on policies, on the constitution, and on the representative system, and succumbed in 1958 in face of a threatened civil war over the status of Algeria.

The factors that determine the precise form of the party structure in any country, together with its stability or instability, are both complex and varied, and stem from history as well as from national temperament. Where, for whatever reason, divisions go too deep to make stable government possible, then there is always a danger that electoral instability will be added to political and constitutional instability. For a party that feels itself wholly out of tune with the country's political life, or feels itself unduly discriminated against in elections, is likely to favour an electoral system that gives it added weight, that is, that strengthens precisely the tendencies already making the system unworkable. The British Liberal Party, apparently in a situation of permanent minority, the French progressive democrat movement, which has felt that anti-clerical elements discriminated against its predominant Catholicism, the French Communist Party, which until recently has rejected the constitutional framework of French republican government—all these have tended to want to replace existing electoral systems by systems of proportional representation in order to strengthen their own position, even at the cost of making the attainment of clear governmental majorities more difficult. In Belgium, the division between French- and Flemish-speaking elements has gone even deeper and now often seems to be a direct threat to the survival of the political system.

In Great Britain and the United States, a number of factors have up to now combined to prevent any deeply divisive quarrel from threatening the political or constitutional framework. The predominance of the Protestant religion, general agreement on the form of government, whether a monarchy or a republic, the absence (at least until very recently) of acute racial problems or of separatist movements of any importance, the domination of industrial interests and the absence of a strong class of 'peasant' farmers, the very longevity of constitutional and political institutions, which in itself increased their stability —all these have helped to make continuously possible the compromises needed for the maintenance of stable party and electoral systems.

Yet even in spite of these advantages, the party system does not give uncritical satisfaction. In both countries, the two main parties have included large and heterogeneous minority interests anxious to press their sectional claims as forcefully as possible within the two-party framework. With the growing complexity of politics and the extension of State activities, sectional interests have grown up that cut across party lines—the interests of car users, for instance, or of professional associations such as the law and medical associations, teachers, women, and so on. In the United States there are special State problems that conflict with general party attitudes. These can be to some extent, though not entirely, catered for by relatively lax party discipline permitting frequent cross-voting in Congress. But parties have come to be increasingly supplemented in their task of reflecting public opinion by interest and pressure groups.

The organisation of these varies a great deal, both within countries and from one country to another. In the United States they are very numerous, and the most powerful of them constitute officially recognized and highly organised bodies equipped to bring strong pressures to bear both on parties and on government departments. In the European Economic Community, the authorities in Brussels keep an official register of recognised interest groups 'at Community level' (that is, representing all six member countries of the E.E.C.). In Great Britain, where party discipline is strict, the activities of lobbies and interest groups are relatively discreet and their real importance often difficult to assess. Moreover, left-wing opinion, with its preference for direct State control over a wider range of industries and services, is traditionally suspicious of pressure groups, regarding them as 'sinister interests' and preferring the direct and open pressures of the main economic interest groups represented by employers' associations and workers' trade unions. In France, on the other hand, with its long history of weak ministries, and its inheritance of centralised administrative structures, there is, at one and the same time, a far wider acceptance than there is in either the United States or Great Britain of government intervention in general in economic life—through the mechanisms of the National Plan, through government aid to producers and through public investment in the private sector—and an acceptance of direct sectional political pressures by lobbies represented in Parliament, either within parliamentary groups, or constituting 'intergroups', cutting across party lines. For instance, in the French Parliament, governments have been regularly subjected to pressures from spokesmen of regional and occupational interests, such as beetroot growers, wine producers (particularly in the south), millers, home distillers, ex-servicemen, as well as to the normal pressures from employers' associations and trade unions.

The Limitations of Representative Democracy

In any country, then, the representative system reflects hopes, desires and dislikes, as well as habits of thought and action that result from its history, as do other political institutions. Even if introduced as an academic blueprint, it takes on a colouring imposed by circumstances and temperament, falling somewhere between what is minimally politically attainable and what is maximally politically desirable. At their best, party organisations are no more than rather clumsy devices for finding some practical way of reducing conflicting opinions to manageable enough proportions to permit of the maintenance of law and order, and the organisation of a country's economic and political life on the basis of the consent of the majority.

There are circumstances in which this purpose can either not be achieved at all, or can be achieved only at the cost of a considerable degree of distortion of opinion. If, for instance, a country is very deeply divided, then, to the extent that the representative system reflects the divisions, it may help to perpetuate them, and so to prevent the possibility of any coherent government. Parties may have to choose, eventually, between their desire to poll their full strength (and the more they are divided, the less likely they are to be prepared to sacrifice some of their voting strength) and their desire to avoid the breakdown of the whole political system. Even in countries with a long history of stable representative and democratic government, it is not easy for a representative system to fulfil with equal success the two functions of representation—to reflect opinion and to provide a government. Great Britain and the United States have both chosen to sacrifice, if necessary, accuracy of representation in order to ensure stable majority government. But they have been able to do this only at the cost of a great deal of compromise within political parties, and of the willingness of defeated parties to accept the verdict of the electorate and sometimes to remain in opposition for a number of years.

Where party divisions are based on some deeply felt constitutional issues, or on political, moral or religious principles such as Protestantism, Catholicism or Marxism, the necessary compromises may not be attainable. In such cases, parties may either prefer to stick to their principles at the cost of remaining permanently in opposition, or be prepared sooner or later to resort to revolutionary methods to obtain power. Where several such parties are opposed to each other as well as to the majority, the consequences can be almost wholly destructive. In the early 1930s, the German Communist Party was able to exploit divisions between Socialists, Conservatives, Liberals and Catholic Centre in order to paralyse democratic government, with the result that Hitler's National Socialist movement was able to destroy the Weimar Republic itself. In the early 1950s, almost half the deputies in the French National Assembly were either Communists or Gaullists. Both these parties were opposed to the whole system of government of the Fourth Republic, but each disliked even more the system desired by the other. The result was that governments could be (and were) defeated by combined Communist and Gaullist votes, though these two parties could not combine to form an alternative government. Successive governments were inevitably coalitions whose political complexion differed very little, since it required almost the whole of the combined strength of the non-Communist and non-Gaullist groups to provide a majority. Governments thus had to limp along as best they could, sometimes having to rely on shifting majorities for different measures, and being reduced to inaction on issues on which no majority at all was forthcoming.

In such circumstances, it is not surprising that the representative system itself should come under fire, although the basic cause of the failure to supply stable government was political division rather than the inadequacies of the party system. At all periods of its history, however, criticisms and doubts of representative systems, or of the way they work, have been expressed by political reformers seeking less imperfect institutions. Rousseau even denied the validity of the whole principle of representation, on the ground that men are unique and cannot be represented. 'The Deputies of the People' [he said] 'are not, nor can they be, its representatives. They can only be its Commissioners. They can make no definite decisions.'[5] Real democratic government would be possible, he thought, only if each citizen were to participate in major political decisions with community and not individual or section interests in mind. He concluded that this would be inconceivable in the world as he knew it. And so, when asked for his advice regarding practical systems of government for Poland and Corsica, he made no attempt to put these theories of direct democracy to the test.

James Madison, one of the founding fathers of the American Constitution, though he shared Rousseau's view that what he called 'pure democracy', in the sense of direct democracy, could not exist in the modern world, did not share Rousseau's pessimism regarding representative government. Indeed, he counted on it as the only means of providing democratic government in modern conditions, and also as a means of overcoming what he saw as one of the chief obstacles to democratic government. This he considered to be 'faction', by which he meant the essential selfishness of sectional interests. 'By faction', [he wrote in 1787] 'I understand a number of citizens whether amounting to a majority or minority of the whole, who are united and actuated by some common impulse of passion, or of interest, or to the permanent and aggregate interests of the community.'[6]

In practice it is impossible to make a clear distinction between faction and party, and the former word tended to be used in the eighteenth century to decry parties, much as some people today use the term 'party-political' in a pejorative sense. Madison's recipe for democracy was what he called 'a republic', by which he meant a system of representative government with built-in safeguards against the dangers of 'faction'. These safeguards were essentially two, first, a large electorate, and second, the federal nature of the American Constitution. The first, up to a certain optimum point, would, in his view, prevent the dominance of any one section and so prevent 'faction', by cancelling out rival sectional interests. By isolating one State from another, the federal constitution would help at least to prevent the spread of 'faction'.

Almost a century later, John Stuart Mill, who also believed in representative government, saw its main weakness in its grant to 'ignorance' of 'as much political power as knowledge'. He was afraid that the democratisation of society might be incompatible with individual distinction. To prevent this from happening, he suggested at least a literacy test for voters. Every elector should, he thought, be able to read, write, and perform the common operations of arithmetic.[7]

These are not the main preoccupations of modern critics of representative democracy. In the modern world, we are much less sure that we can discover any objective criteria of either the public good or desirable qualifications. In any case, the increasing pace of twentieth-century decolonisation has brought universal suffrage to large numbers of new States in which illiteracy is the rule rather than the exception. And the growth of party organisation, together with the modern paraphernalia of mass media, has provided new techniques of persuasion and pressure, which can reach almost all sections of the public, in one form or another. Modern doubts and criticisms are concerned more with the possibilities of improving the techniques of consultation, in the hope of finding ways of recording opinions more accurately without having to pay the price of governmental instability.

Experience does not suggest that representative institutions, though they can sometimes secure a victory for one party or one alliance in a particular election, can be counted on to mould political systems permanently. If, as has been suggested, they are the product of political habits and circumstances, then their influence could hardly be expected to be formative. A nation does not owe stable government to its representative or its parliamentary system. It is likely to have stable institutions if it is a politically stable country. Where institutions can help, and representative systems in particular, is in strengthening existing trends. Insofar as electoral and party systems become generally accepted by the public as part of a settled way of life, they help to increase stability by the very fact that one of the most fruitful sources of discord is removed from the political stage. The fact that, in both the United States and Great Britain, government and opposition are equally convinced of the benefits of a two-party system helps to maintain it, and to encourage the political attitudes enabling it to function efficiently—the readiness to compromise, the desire not to embitter inter-party strife more than necessary, the refusal to abuse the accepted constitutional and procedural rules of the game, and so on. But if these attitudes were to change under the stress of circumstances, then it would be unrealistic to count on the party system to remain immune from the danger of political instability.

There are a number of ways in which a representative system can become vulnerable. A two-party system can become too rigid and too in-turned and so become unrepresentative of public opinion without the leaders being aware of the fact.

Such a situation could present serious dangers because the very size and resources of parties, where there are only two, virtually rule out the possibility of their being effectively challenged by new third parties, except over a very long period of time. In a multi-party system, where party organisations are smaller and more numerous, not only is movement between them sometimes easier (particularly where there are no fundamental doctrinal or religious differences), but the financial problems of forming breakaway groups are often much less formidable. One of the main dangers of multi-party systems is, indeed, too small and too short-lived parties. But too large parties can become too long-lived, and their eventual adjustment to changing circumstances be achieved only at the cost of painful dislocation.

There are also some apparently inherent weaknesses in party structures today. One is the imbalance created by the fact that some interests are more easily and, therefore, more effectively organised than others. If, as has been argued, pressure groups play a valuable part in organising public opinion, the pressure exerted is far from evenly spread over the different sectors. For example, the two main economic pressure groups, those of employers and workers, both represent producers, and can often have more interests in common with each other than either has with consumers. Miners are a recognisable category with basically similar interests. Users of coal are not. Building firms and their workers share an interest in the profitability of the firm and the industry, even though they may frequently differ regarding the way the profits ought to be distributed. The interest of house purchasers are in conflict with those of builders, but they have no comparable organisation through which they can exert pressure.

Many sections of the community have, thus, to rely entirely on political parties to represent their interests, because, as Sartori puts it, 'the average voter does not act, he reacts'.[8] The difference between an efficient and an inefficient democracy will depend in great measure on the extent to which electoral and party machinery helps to increase the number of actors and diminish the number of reactors. But however well-organised they may be, parties and pressure groups must remain essentially clumsy and imperfect organs both for eliciting opinions and for maintaining an effective dialogue between

government and governed or between party leadership and
its rank and file. In the last resort, the quality of representative
institutions must reflect the quality of citizenship.

> Representative institutions [said John Stuart Mill] necessarily
> depend for permanence upon the readiness of the people
> to fight for them in case of their being endangered. If too
> little valued for this, they seldom obtain a footing at all, and
> if they do, are almost sure to be overthrown, as soon as the
> head of the government, or any party leader who can muster
> force for a *coup de main,* is willing to run some small risk
> for absolute power. . . .
> . . . When nobody, or only some small fraction, feels the
> degree of interest in the general affairs of the State necessary
> to the formation of a public opinion, the electors will seldom
> make any use of the right of suffrage but to serve their private
> interest or the interest of their locality. . . .[9]

Whether parties and electoral systems are good or bad, however, no democratic system has up to now found a satisfactory
substitute for them.

> If parties cause some evils [wrote Bryce] they avert or mitigate
> others. To begin with, parties are inevitable. No free large
> country has been without them. They bring order out of
> the chaos of a multitude of voters. If in such vast populations
> as those of the United States, France or England, there were
> no party organisations, by whom would public opinion be
> roused and educated to certain specific purposes? Each party,
> no doubt, tries to present its own side of the case for or
> against any doctrine or proposal, but the public cannot help
> learning something about the other side also, for even party
> spirit cannot separate the nation into water-tight compart-
> ments; and the most artful or prejudiced party spellbinder
> or newspaper has to recognise the existence of the arguments
> he is trying to refute. Thus party strife is a sort of education
> for those willing to receive instruction, and something soaks
> through even into the less interested or thoughtful electors.
> The parties keep a nation's mind alive, as the rise and fall of
> the sweeping tide freshens the water of long ocean inlets.[10]

4

Political Democracy

Democracy is a system of government according to which every member of a society is considered as a man and nothing more.
William Godwin, An Enquiry Concerning Democracy

The democrat as such is only concerned with economic inequalities in so far as they do in fact militate against the successful working of democracy . . . . It would be legitimate, therefore, for the democrat to hold the view that it is better to forego the measure of improvement which the achievement of economic equality might render possible in the working of the democratic method. The desirability or otherwise of economic equality is, in fact, just as much a subject of controversy among those who accept democratic methods as it is among those who do not.
Reginald Bassett, The Essentials of Parliamentary Democracy

So far, then, from economics importing its own planned system into politics, it is the business of politics to import a planned system into economics. But the plan which politics has to introduce is not an economic plan. It is a political plan. In other words, it is a plan for adjusting those claims and counter-claims of right which affect the whole political community.
Ernest Barker, Reflections on Government

Civil liberties aim at the protection of the individual against authority; political democracy aims at the just and rational organization of authority in human society.
Leonard Woolf, After the Deluge

Liberal Democracy

For most of the nineteenth century, democracy in Great Britain and the United States continued to be regarded predominantly in political and legal terms, that is, in terms of a gradual extension of the franchise and of a system of justice making possible the kind of rule of law defined by Dicey. Many people did not believe, either in the need for, or the desirability of, universal suffrage. Hardly anybody believed that the kind of democracy expected from a representative political system either would or should include economic or social egalitarianism, much less the substitution for liberal democracy of any system that could legitimately be described as Socialist.

Liberal democracy* was still based on certain widely held, underlying assumptions, not necessarily compatible with each other. There was still a conscious or unconscious acceptance of Adam Smith's belief in a natural economic order, attainable by the free play of economic forces. This implied that the role of the State should be seen as little more than that of maintaining order and of providing a minimum of general and coordinating regulations, forming a framework within which these economic forces could fulfil their own role of harmonising conflicting interests. There must, for instance, be an independent and just legal system capable of stepping in and settling such of these differences as proved in practice not to be amenable to settlement by 'a balance between conflicting greeds and errors'.[1]

This assumption that 'God's in his heaven, all's right with the world' had already been dramatically shaken in Great Britain by the upheavals produced by the industrial revolution. A period of violent changes had reduced large sections of the population to poverty and unemployment, while some individuals and classes had climbed rapidly to situations of great economic power. The social unrest and the social problems created by poverty and squalor had showed up both the unreality of theories of natural harmony and the inadequacies of private charity. Insanitary conditions, bad housing, poverty and ignorance were coming to be seen as social diseases, that is diseases inherent in the form of society itself, and that could not be remedied by individual action, but only by changes in society, and whose effects could not be confined to one class of society. Without positive action by governments, the poverty and disease of some would constitute a threat to all. The second half of the century, therefore, saw the development of intervention by government and local authorities in many social fields. The content of the notion of liberal democracy was rapidly changing, by general consent and with a minimum of ideological conflict.

*The word 'liberal' is used in this chapter with a small 'l' when it refers to liberalism in any party. When the Liberal Party or its policy is referred to, the capital letter is used.

Pressures for the extension of the suffrage, together with the growth of radical reform movements, began to challenge other comfortable illusions on which representative government had been built up, namely, the assumptions that private property, the coexistence of rich and poor, and a general acceptance of the right and duty of the better educated to govern in the interests of all were part of the permanent order of things. This view was already beginning to be challenged by Socialists of all brands, but in Great Britain Socialism made little impact until well into the twentieth century, the influence of Marxism was late in making itself felt and has always been small. As late as 1920, Lord Bryce expressed the view, with which few of his compatriots would have quarreled, that, democracy, since it is 'merely a form of Government, not a consideration of the purposes to which government may be turned, has nothing to do with economic equality.'[2]

If he meant that economic equality was not a necessary condition of democratic government, then the statement was unchallengeable, for the simple reasons that the term 'economic equality' has never had any precise meaning. Nor has it ever been clear how far whatever principles the term can be held to embody at any particular moment of time and in any particular country can be translated into practice by political means. If, however, he meant to imply that, in political democracies, people would not sooner or later come to regard gross disparities of economic and social opportunity as obstacles to the efficient working of democratic institutions, then he was clearly in error.

It is nevertheless necessary to make a clear distinction between theories claiming that democracy is incomplete or inefficient without an economic and social as well as a political and legal content and those that postulate as one of the objectives of democracy the attainment of complete economic equality. Notwithstanding seventeenth- and eighteenth-century myths regarding the existence of a primitive age of innocence when equality was the rule, and twentieth-century myths regarding the possibility of moving rapidly towards classless societies, the rule in all known civilised and uncivilised societies has been that of inequality. As Tawney put it, 'Inequality is easy, since it demands no more than to float with the current, equality is difficult for it involves swimming against it.'[3] Which is merely another way of saying that, as far as we know, most people do not want equality and classlessness. Since democracy is based on the thesis that the criterion of political action is what the majority want, 'swimming against the current' must imply, either that equality is to be imposed against the will of the majority, or that it is likely to remain only a distant theoretical goal, or else that it is a principle to which lip service is paid without any illusions that much can be done to implement it.

It does not follow, however, that, because it is not possible to give a positive content to the concept of equality that is capable of being translated into political programmes, the only alternative is to fall back on nineteenth-century concepts of legal and political democracy. Unfortunately it is also true that, as positive ideals, political liberty and legal equality are no less imprecise and subjective, and therefore undefinable and unattainable. Both the American and British systems became liberal democracies, less by concentrating on contested and ill-defined ends than by seeking agreed solutions to empirically recognised problems. The criteria on which decisions have been based have never been either logical or consistent. But the electors have been periodically consulted on them, and required to decide for or against whatever decisions have been taken, or are to be taken, by governments.

However necessary and desirable it may be for political thinkers to discuss general principles, and for politicians to be aware of the philosophical uncertainties and divergences which underly their positive decisions, politics must be concerned above all with action, and it is quite possible—and often necessary—to take a series of practical steps along a road, without necessarily knowing either exactly where it is leading or whether it will ever be possible to know where it may lead, just as it is possible for any reasonably intelligent elector to decide for himself whether or not he thinks it right for an accused person to be kept in custody for days, weeks or months before being brought to trial, or whether, on the basis of evidence, a particular offender is or is not fit to be allowed to drive a car. It is much more difficult to define the positive principles that should govern the relationship between crime and punishment. Except in cases where the continuity of political life is broken by, for instance, revolution or by a sudden fundamental change in political attitudes or economic or political circumstances, most political decisions are concerned with the rate of advance along a road already being travelled. They are mainly concerned with questions of more or less, and the answers are determined by the whole complex of laws, customs, religion and morals that go to make up the political climate of the time.

The content of general concepts such as liberty, equality and justice, then, will evolve in the light of climates that are perpetually changing in response to the challenge of whatever are the burning issues of the time. Those who drew up the American Declaration of Independence stated their belief that '... all men are created equal; that they are endowed by their Creator with certain inalienable rights; that among these are life, liberty and the pursuit of happiness. ...' Though they wrote in general terms, their attention was fixed on particular rights and liberties that were in the forefront of American minds at that time. When, in 1789, the French Revolutionaries proclaimed in article 1 of the Declaration of the Rights of Man and the Citizen that 'men are born and remain free and equal in rights', they were not proclaiming their belief in complete legal, political or social equality, but only in those aspects of equality that most exercised their minds at the time. They were objecting primarily to the right of the sovereign to imprison citizens arbitrarily without a fair trial, to the fact that the ruler was able to treat himself as being above the law, and to the existence of legal and financial privileges enjoyed by the aristocracy and the Church.

Beneath these doctrinal approaches to politics, there is also a strong pragmatic element, and pragmatism is one of the essential characteristics of liberal democracy. But it can work well only if there exists an adequte framework of generally accepted political institutions and habits, and if neither too many nor too complex demands are made on a mass electorate. It was within such a framework that Macaulay could describe the principle of British parliamentary government as being the predominance of the practical element over the speculative.

The perfect lawgiver [he said] is a just temper between the mere man of theory, who can see nothing but general principles, and the mere man of business who can see nothing but particular circumstances. Of lawgivers in whom the speculative element has prevailed to the exclusion of the practical, the world has during the last eighty years been singularly fruit-

ful. To their wisdom Europe and America have owed scores
of abortive constitutions, scores of constitutions which have
lived just long enough to make a miserable noise, and have
then gone off in convulsions. But in British legislation the
practical element has always predominated and not seldom
unduly predominated over the speculative. To think nothing
of symmetry and much of convenience; never to remove an
anomaly merely because it is an anomaly; never to innovate
except when some grievance is felt; never to innovate except
so far as to get rid of the grievance; never to lay down any
proposition of wider extent than the particular case for which
it is necessary to provide; these are the rules which have,
from the age of John to the age of Victoria, generally guided
the deliberations of our two hundred and fifty parliaments.
Our national distaste for whatever is abstract in political
science amounts undoubtedly to a fault. Yet it is, perhaps,
a fault on the right side.[4]

It would be impossible to defend this degree of pragmatism
today, and it was already becoming out of date in Great Britain
before the death of Victoria. National economic planning, and
massive State intervention in social as well as economic matters,
which are now accepted in practice, and in some considerable
degree, even in the most 'capitalist' countries, have entailed
an ever-increasing flow of legislation and administrative orders,
on a scale undreamed of in Macaulay's day. Coordination and
consistency in legislation and in governmental and party programmes are essential, and so is thinking ahead, with a view to
preventing Parliament from being snowed under by too many
anomalies. But where constitutional and political differences
are neither wide nor deep, it is still possible to maintain a pragmatic approach. In matters concerning interpretations of principles such as individual liberty and economic and social inequality, on which liberal democrats assume that there will never
be agreement, there is something to be said for the spirit of
caution and compromise with which the Toleration Act (which
was what Macaulay was talking about) was approached. It succeeded, he believed, in 'removing a mass of evil without shocking
a vast mass of prejudice', and without laying down any general
principle intended to tie the hands of legislators in any future
controversy.

E

The method is open to at least two major criticisms. It is possible only in the kind of climate that has existed hitherto in Great Britain and America, that is, one of consensus politics, in which give and take have been possible within a commonly accepted political and economic framework. Though there were relatively bitter arguments in Great Britain over economic policies such as nationalisation and social security, they never went deep enough either to threaten the political system or to make one side set out systematically to undo what had been done by the other. This amounts to postulating as a condition of effective liberal democracy that it should already exist and be working relatively well, in order to be proof against the stresses and strains of political or economic controversy. As Sir Denis Brogan has put it

> What we have to accept is that in England, historical habit, more than legal or political doctrine, conditions the practice of citizenship, explains the claims made and not made, the duties accepted and not accepted ... and there is in the national temper a great deal of that conservatism, described in the maxim of academic politics laid down, ironically, by F. M. Cornford: 'Nothing should ever be done for the first time'.[5]

Perhaps what conditions the practice of citizenship in America is not so much political as constitutional habit. But whatever it is, the resulting Anglo-Saxon climate is one that has so far made the pragmatic approach of liberal democracy possible. In France, on the other hand, where both historical habits and legal and political doctrines have formed different attitudes to problems of citizenship and consensus, there have been occasions where the conditions for the effective working of liberal democracy were simply not present. In such circumstances, the role of system-making and ideology tends in any case to be greater, and even more so since, for many reasons, the attraction of theory and doctrine is much greater in France than it has ever been in Anglo-Saxon and Scandinavian countries.

The second criticism, which is peculiarly pertinent to some of the present-day strains in democratic systems that are discussed in the last chapter, is that the pragmatic approach is very slow and undramatic and, therefore, lacks popular appeal, especially to the young in an age of more rapid economic and technical change than man has ever known. It is intellectually, no doubt, more satisfying to think of today's tremendous problems in terms of wholesale and rapid change, of revolution and fresh starts, particularly as it is more and more difficult in modern conditions to find adequate techniques for public participation in decision making, without gravely reducing efficiency. If society cannot be changed fast enough to satisfy the majority by the slow and piecemeal methods of liberal democracy, then, sooner or later, there will inevitably be pressure for more radical methods. It is noteworthy that one of the most obvious responses today to the problems of adapting democratic methods to the age of the computer and the H-bomb has been the growth of political attitudes expressing impatience with established democratic procedures, and desires for more dramatic forms of political action. And these attitudes have developed in the oldest and most stable democracies, as well as in the newer and less settled systems.

Liberal Democracy and Democratic Socialism

There is, in theory, a clear line separating liberal democracy from democratic Socialism, in that the latter advocates, in principle at least, the collective ownership or control of the most important means of production, distribution and exchange, while for the former the principle of private enterprise remains the general rule. For purposes of practical politics the division is often less simple. The Socialist goal is a long-term one. Liberal democrats have increasingly been obliged to accept, or have themselves proposed, State intervention, including a measure of public control. They have done so either in order to protect individuals and sections of society from the more evident evils of unfettered private enterprise, or merely in the interests of greater efficiency. The differences, therefore, in terms of practical policies between Socialist and liberal democratic governments, at least in Anglo-Saxon and Scandinavian countries, have often been mainly those of emphasis, of more or less, of ends rather than means. Where liberal democrats have emphasised individual freedom and demanded that the State shall not lose sight of this in the search for social justice, Socialists have emphasised social interests, and demanded that these shall take precedence where social and private needs are in conflict. Liberal democrats have been prepared, in case of doubt as to where to draw the line, to accept a greater degree of inequality or privilege in order to safeguard individual freedom. The desire to end privilege has sometimes led Socialists to accept—and even to welcome—a degree of uniformity that can be achieved only by the imposition by the State of restrictions that, to some liberals, appear unjustified.

The question of the control of the economy through collective ownership or through planning has often been a touchstone. The principle of private enterprise, approved by conservative and liberal opinion and rejected by Communists, has been for Socialists essentially a matter of more or less. Where the proportion of small-property holders (including peasant farmers and small businesses) has been high, the Socialist view has amounted to approval of small and condemnation of large concerns. In France, even the Communist Party has never felt able to come out openly in favour of nationalisation of the land. Indeed, it has often gone out of its way to campaign for the votes of peasant farmers by slogans such as 'the land for the peasants'. Some Socialists support policies often described as 'economic democracy', by which they mean the desirability of applying democratic methods to the economic field, by devices ranging from simple consultation of workers to some measure of direct participation in management. But it must be added that some non-Socialists also advocate such schemes, while some Socialists see them as devices intended to turn the thoughts of the workers away from more fundamental economic and social changes.

Socialists are agreed, however, not only in advocating democratic methods, but also in their general purpose. Whether they approve of more or less economic intervention by the State, involving restrictions on individual freedom of action, they see such intervention as seeking to increase freedom, in the sense of enlarging the scope of individual opportunities, and also as seeking to eliminate progressively inequalities between citizens. There is, then, room for a wide range of opinions within the framework of liberal democracy, taking in political conservatism and radical reformism as well as democratic Socialism, by which is understood a Socialist system arrived at by constitutional and legal methods, and sharing liberal views regarding the basic individual freedoms of opinion, assembly and association.

British Pragmatic Reformism

Before the end of the nineteenth century, some reformist movements in Great Britain had already come to believe that the
only effective way to get a truly liberal democracy would be to
reform society along Socialist lines. Their supporters remained
'liberals' in the sense that they advocated only peaceful and
constitutional methods of persuasion. They were 'gradualist',
believing that the transition to Socialism should be made without
any dislocation of national life, and so could come only slowly
(hence the fact that one of the most influential of these movements described itself as Fabian), by the eventual conver-
sion of the majority to Socialism, and in the interim period by a
kind of osmosis enabling Socialist principles to permeate existing
parties. They conceived of Socialism primarily in terms of the
extension of public control, either by the State or by local authorities.

Since Socialism was seen as attainable only at the end of a
long road of progressive reforms, there remained a wide area
within which the immediate interests of Socialists did not
diverge from those of radical liberal opinion. There was, indeed, practicable cooperation in the House of Commons between
Liberals and the small Labour Party formed at the beginning
of the century. It was not until 1918 that the British Labour
Party, in which the reformist trade-union element has always
been dominant, formally described itself as Socialist. And it was
not until 1945 that a Labour government was able to carry out
the first application of the Socialist principle of public control
of large areas of economic life.

The convergence of practical and immediate interests should
not, however, be allowed to obscure the essential divergences
that separate radical liberals from liberal Socialists. There is a
basic Socialist assumption that it is possible to harmonise social
and individual needs, that State intervention and public ownership will positively increase individual freedom, and, therefore,
help to promote democracy by eliminating poverty and dis-
abilities imposed by lack of educational or social opportunity,
or by gross inequalities of wealth, and at the same time ensure
more efficient running of the country in the interests of the
whole community. This assumption is not made by liberal
democrats. Even though they may accept restraints on the indi-

vidual in the interests of society as a whole, State control has been seen as restricting the individual rather than freeing him. But the fact that there is never likely to be agreement on the precise points at which the claims of society should have priority over those of the individual, if it proves in practice impossible to reconcile the two, has tended to produce changing emphases at different times in Socialist and non-Socialist liberal thought. There is no reason to assume that this process will not go on, and that the two tendencies will not be sometimes nearer to each other, and sometimes farther apart.

The present tendency is for them to be closer to each other in ideas, though not in political temperament and habit. In the late 1960s, the outlook of many Socialists was changing in two main ways. First, they were questioning the advisability of any considerable extension of the policy of direct national-isation of industries, and concentrating more attention on plan-ning, on various forms of indirect control of private enterprise, and on possible forms of cooperation between public and private sectors. Second, they were beginning to realise that the growth of vast monopolies, whether State-controlled or private, could involve a degree of bureaucracy and of remoteness from the ordinary citizen that made him feel less free than hitherto. There was a growing recognition of the need for more effective rep-resentation of the views of consumers within the State-controlled industries and services, for better ways of enabling consumers to judge the merits and demerits of goods produced, whether by private or by public concerns, and for effective control of, or appeal from, the more and more numerous decisions taken by officials. The growth of administrative tribunals (and the criticisms of their working), the appointment by a Labour govern-ment of an Ombudsman, and public demands for similar pro-tection from the arbitrary decisions of local officials, all indi-cated the growing anxiety among Socialists, as well as in the other parties, lest State services, such as those of health, educa-tion and the nationalised industries, together with the increasing size of industrial concerns, should lead to the development of inadequately controlled bureaucracies.

At the same time, British liberal opinion was also reassessing its principles in the light of the changing economic and tech-nological conditions. For instance, a Liberal Party report pub-lished in 1969 came out strongly in favour of extensive State intervention, not merely as a regrettable necessity, but as a positive means of reducing social and economic inequalities, and of improving the quality of individual freedom. There was an acceptance of the socialist assumption that 'communal duty and individual independence' must be reconciled, and an expression of Liberal willingness to introduce reforms 'more revolutionary in their implications than any Socialist dreams of, and defences for achievements of the past deeper than any Tory dares to demand'.[6]

There is, therefore, considerable scope for rapprochement between Liberal and Socialist *policies* in Great Britain, particularly in an age in which so many accepted ideas and traditions are undergoing extensive rethinking. But this by no means implies that non-Socialist and Socialist political parties will merge. The boundaries between them are not clearcut, but they exist, and they are reinforced by the fact that each has its moderate and its more extreme wing or wings, and that the extremes within each party find any close or lasting cooperation with liberal elements in any other distasteful. Three characteristics of British Socialism, in particular, have, however, up to now helped to prevent the degree of separation between Socialist and non-Socialist liberal opinion that has often existed in continental democratic systems, and these have also helped to increase the separation between British Socialist and Communist Parties. They are the negligible influence of Marxist theories, the common background of Protestantism, and perhaps especially of Methodism, and, most important of all, the predominant interest of liberal opinion in all three British parties in practical reforms, instead of in the doctrinal issues that have so often torn continental progressive parties apart.

American Liberal Democracy

In the United States, neither Socialism nor Communism has ever attracted much support. Until very recently, America has been regarded by citizens and immigrants alike as being, *par excellence,* the country that combined free enterprise and individual opportunity. It is true that, for some, freedom has meant poverty and that, for the rapidly growing Negro population, America has provided fewer opportunities than for the rest. But life for American Negroes has still compared favourably with the situation of Negroes almost anywhere else. And for the millions of refugees from Europe, the United States has been a 'new world' that offered them, first, land and economic freedom as well as freedom of political opinion, and, later, as a minimum, freedom of opinion, together with reasonable economic opportunities.

The American democratic tradition has three important characteristics, absent from the British and French traditions. The first is consciousness of a revolutionary heritage that is quite different from that of the French. There is certainly a kind of nostalgic affinity between American and French Republicans, mainly restricted to intellectual circles, and deriving both from the common feeling of having had to fight for national freedom, and from the image of Republicanism as a system without class privilege or a hereditary aristocracy. But whereas the French Revolution was a civil war that began by dividing Frenchmen and still does divide them, the American Revolution was a foreign war, and foreign wars unite. The American Revolution still does unite American parties, whose political dialogue is one of differing degrees of liberalism, and of differing emphases, often less perceptible to outsiders than to Americans. In practical politics, the Democratic Party is more inclined to favour federal intervention in economic and social fields, readier to accept working-class claims for improved conditions, and to see the trade union point of view, and more sympathetic (except in the Southern States) to Negro claims for equality. The Republican Party is more associated with big business, less willing to spend on public services, more suspicious of organised Labour, more isolationist.

But what unites Democrats and Republicans goes far deeper than what separates them. And nothing makes this clearer than the four-yearly presidential campaign, in which policies are never clearly differentiated and even shades of difference are often obliterated or forgotten once the campaign is over. As a commentator remarked during the 1960 presidential election campaign: '... many people inside and outside the United States must be wondering what the election is about. Both parties apparently stand for the same policies: both are for economic growth and a vigorous defence policy: both are against racial segregation and sin.'[7] Or as Alistair Cooke put it during the same campaign·

... a platform is not for running on. ... It is rather like the marriage service. It does not remotely describe the way the marriage came about. It defines a contract that the couple must swear to, but the literal prescriptions of the contract are rarely brought up again except as grounds for divorce. Once the bridegroom is picked, he can forget it, [i.e. the contract or party programme] enforce its exact opposite (as Franklin Roosevelt notoriously did in 1933), and write his own ticket.[8]

The second characteristic is the diffusion of authority that comes in the first place from a federal system in which the States not only have the residual powers, but have in many cases first claims on the loyalty of politicians as well as of ordinary citizens. Senators are elected to represent their States, Members of the House of Representatives must be residents of their constituency. The focus of politics is concentrated at one extreme on the central federal figure, the President, and at the other, on the local representative. There is in the United States no equivalent of the French and British conception of the State. And this diffusion of political authority is increased by the absence of racial and cultural homogeneity resulting from large-scale and continuous immigration.

It can be asked why this should be so, when the Swiss Confederation can claim to have successfully welded toegether in one nation three major national cultures, together with three national languages and one dialect. But Switzerland is a small country, and one that has been throughout much of her history more isolated from her neighbours than other European countries, because of mountain barriers; a country, moreover, whose different nationalities all share West-European traditions and cultures, and which has had a long federal history. America is a continent. The racial and linguistic differences are numerous. The immigrants have come from a wide range of countries and are still coming, even if the rate has slowed down to a comparative trickle during the present century. It is all recent enough for Americans to feel themselves 'dominated by the spectre of known foreign ancestors',[9] and for them to have become obsessed with a parental image that is a kind of oscillation between ancestor-worship and ancestor-resentment. What this has meant in political terms is that the focus of unity that, both in France and England, comes from the sense of being old countries with long histories as nation-States is lacking in American society, and this has helped to strengthen State loyalities and to stiffen resistance to the modern tendency towards the transfer of State responsibilities to the Federal authorities.

The constitution, as has so often been said, has replaced the nation as the symbol of American unity. This is the third characteristic, and one that it is essential to understand in order to understand American democracy. The constitution is an unwieldy, anachronistic document that has had to be made to work by the conscious efforts of successive generations of statesmen, and by continuous, ingenious, and often tortuous interpretations and reinterpretations of its provisions by generations of lawyers, complemented by a few—very few—formal amendments to the document itself. The whole process would never have been possible, if it had not been for the attachment of the American people to what it stands for. The French, on the other hand, who appear to have drawn up every one of their many constitutions with the implicit—and sometimes explicit —purpose of legislating for all time, have produced, at most, only one Republican constitution that could claim to have achieved, for a few years, the distinction of being regarded by (almost) all Frenchmen as likely to be permanent.

This general agreement in the United States on the political structure has been accompanied by general agreement on economic policies, at least until very recently. A description of American society at the beginning of this century, noted that 'Worker, farmer and proper Bostonian were all democratic capitalists'[10] and that economic liberalism was so universal that it could be taken for granted. Political stability and economic opportunity, together with comparative remoteness from the international troubles of Europe, except during the periods when Americans were actually fighting in two world wars, have combined to make this description almost as true of the 1960s. But American liberal democracy has not only meant political stability and economic opportunity. It has also meant (at least up to the later years of the Vietnam war, and the coming of racial violence) an absence of ideological controversy, a general optimism regarding the possibility of economic and social progress, and a general belief in the rightness of American political and economic methods and the assured position of America in the world.

The French Revolutionary Tradition

It has been possible to discuss the democratic tradition in America and Great Britain almost wholly in the context of 'freedom broadening down from precedent to precedent', of dialogue and peaceful change, because the debt that both democracies owe to revolution—the 'bloodless' revolution of 1688, and the American war of independence—is so much smaller than the debt that French democracy owes—and, more important, feels that it owes—to the French Revolution. Both Anglo-Saxon countries already had settled systems of government which, though not then democratic, enabled the changes imposed by their respective revolutions to be absorbed and the systems modified, in ways that helped to make them eventually fully democratic. In European countries such as Germany, Italy, and above all France, democratic government came later and, in all three, there have been periods when it has been replaced for shorter or longer periods by some form of non-democratic rule. For different reasons, all three have failed to create the kind of unquestioned and stable loyalty to a particular constitution that has up to now characterised the consensus politics of the two Anglo-Saxon democracies.

In France, the transition from absolute monarchy to a régime intended to be built on the principles of liberty, equality and fraternity was sudden and violent. It created tremendous hopes, followed within a short time by disappointment and disillusionment. The revolutionaries had to fight a war as well as to wrestle with the totally unfamiliar problem of establishing a new régime. The revolution had been inspired by theories, but the revolutionaries had no practical experience of representative government or, indeed, of any kind of government, and so made elementary mistakes—such as, for instance, deciding that members of the Constituent Assembly should not sit in that elected in 1791, which meant that they deprived themselves at one blow of all the politicians who had acquired the beginnings of an understanding of practical politics.

The reaction against revolutionary excesses led to almost a century of constitutional experiment. In 1869, Léon Gambetta, the founder of French Radicalism, was still fighting for a democratic régime. A properly constituted and honest democracy, he said to his electors in Belleville, is

> the political system which, *par excellence,* leads with the greatest speed and certainty to the moral and material emancipation of the greatest number, and which best ensures social equality in law, in fact, and in custom … the gradual achievement of these social reforms is completely dependent on the kind of régime and on political reforms.[11]

During the long period of alternating authoritarian régimes and brief democratic or Socialist revolutions, however, a revolutionary tradition had been built up. It was expressed by the inclusion of the principles of the 1789 Declaration of the Rights of Man and the Citizen either in the preamble or the text of a number of the democratic and republican constitutions drawn up over those eighty years. And among those principles there is the recognition of 'resistance to oppression' as a 'natural and imprescriptible right'. The Jacobin constitution of 1793 went even farther, and claimed that 'when the Government violates the rights of the people', 'insurrection' is 'the most sacred right and the most indispensable duty'.[12]

This right is, to be sure, always hedged about with conditions, though these are so vaguely and confusingly formulated as to supply little real guidance. It has become now-a-days little more than a nostalgic myth. But the character of a political system is partly determined by its myths and attitudes, and the influence of this revolutionary tradition has been responsible for political attitudes sometimes very far removed from the constitutional and legalistic reformism of British and American pragmatic democracy. French opinion has been, and still is, more tolerant than British opinion (up to the advent of the anarchist and 'hippy' phenomena) of some degree of violence in the expression of political protest. There has been a special tolerance of student direct action, a sentimental acceptance of 'fighting on the barricades' that is a direct heritage of generations of memories of political revolutions, beginning with that of 1789, that have been fought out in the Paris streets. In 1936, there was widespread acceptance of a partial general strike, called *after* the formation, following an electoral victory, of a Popular Front government representing the views of the strikers, because this was seen as a legitimate adjunct to the regular machinery of the ballot-box—a way of strengthening the hand of the government. In 1968, there were a number of French democrats (not all of them Socialists) who were able to persuade themselves for a few days that a progressive government could be helped into power by a revolutionary battle fought in the streets, without recognised leaders, without agreed principles, and without any agreed political programme.

Even as convinced a constitutional democrat as Léon Blum believed as late as the 1930s that there would be at least a revolutionary element in the transition from capitalism to Socialism. There would be, he thought, a brief period during which existing law would no longer be recognised. He described this as *les vacances de la légalité*, a legal vacuum, during which the revolutionary power of the people would be the effective law. The supreme importance attached to 'the voice of the people' is, indeed, the essential justification of the revolutionary right to revolt. It can be used, too, as a justification for overriding regular democratic and constitutional procedures. In 1962, many people believed that a constitutional amendment providing for the President to be elected by universal suffrage was itself unconstitutional. Nevertheless, once it had been accepted by 'the sovereign people' in a referendum, it was generally regarded as having been legitimised by a higher authority than the written constitution.

The revolutionary tradition has also been responsible for a much greater emphasis in French than in British democracy on the principle of equality. The 1789 Declaration of the Rights of Man not only held all men to be equal before the law, but also stated that social distinctions should be determined on the basis of their utility to the community, and that all citizens should be equally eligible for 'honours, office, and positions in public employment' on the sole basis of merit. It was in order to safeguard this last right that, in the early years of this century, a unified educational system was introduced under Radical inspiration, and democratised a quarter of a century later, under Radical and Socialist inspiration. It has contributed a great deal to the ability of French citizens to choose a career in whatever field they choose, on the basis of educational attainment and intellectual merit. It has not produced a classless society, and it was not intended to do so. Nor has the State's refusal to recognise hereditary titles prevented them from being widely used and from helping to perpetuate social distinctions. The French can be socially as class-conscious as the British are accused of being (though in very different ways).

The revolutionary tradition has, however, helped to create a widespread feeling, difficult to define, though easily recognised by anyone familiar with French political attitudes. It is the kind of sentiment so admirably described by Alain, whose village craftsman was able to 'accept the fact that the rich wear out the road with their cars, but not that they should call themselves masters, but who, precisely because inequality was everywhere, insisted that "the principle of equality be proclaimed loud and clear".'[13] This is not the economic or social egalitarianism that is discussed in the next chapter. It is not even the affirmation of the moral equality expressed in the phrase 'a man's a man for a' that'. It is essentially the assertion of a political equality, originally recognised in the Declaration of the Rights of Man and the Citizen as being conferred by the common dignity of citizenship, which has made French democracy consciously and deliberately that of a politically non-deferential people.

5
'Economic' and 'Social' Democracy

There is an instinctive refusal in these Marxist days to accept non-economic causes for political events. . . . But it is a delusion to think that when the economy is as healthy as it can be, and opportunity is equal, everyone will be content.

Leonard Beaton, The Times, 13 September 1968.

. . . in the name of equality two opposite solutions are favoured: the one which asks for an equality that respects diversity; and the other that sees inequality in every diversity; the one which repudiates privileged differences in order to promote the authentic ones, and the other which rejects any difference whatsoever. . . .

Giovanni Sartori, Democratic Theory

. . . in order to secure what is called 'real' or 'true' or 'pure' democracy, i.e. all kinds of things having no necessary connection with the democratic method, some people will actually advocate the methods of violent revolution and dictatorship. . . . To get 'economic democracy', i.e. economic equality, people will advocate policies which, in fact, involve the abandonment of democracy as a political method. Thus we have the paradoxical position that democracy is attacked in the name of 'democracy', and sometimes sacrificed to the achievement of 'democracy'.

Reginald Bassett, The Essentials of Parliamentary Democracy

Is There Such a Thing as 'Economic Democracy'?

In what has been described as liberal democracy, whether the principles by which it is inspired are those of Conservatism, Liberalism, or Socialism, the extent of economic and social levelling is ultimately decided, like anything else, by the electors. As on any other subject, there are wide differences of opinion, both within any democratic system and between one system and another, on the extent to which, and the ways in which, economic and social disadvantages ought to be eliminated in the interests of justice, stability, popularity, efficiency or individual freedom, as well as on whether they can ever be eliminated. It has often been claimed, however, that democracy is merely a façade, unless it is based on the acceptance of the objectives of economic and social equality. Since there is no agreed definition of what these principles mean in political terms, which is what national governments must be concerned with, it is only too easy for discussion on how a democratic system works, or ought to work, to slip into dreams about what an ideal system would be like, irrespective of the means available to achieve these ideals. The process leads to a proliferation of adjectives which, in themselves, supply eloquent evidence of the confusion of thought on these very vague and ambiguous concepts. Democracy is sometimes condemned as 'capitalist', 'political', or 'class-conscious', or it is praised as 'socialist', 'economic', 'popular' or 'classless', according to the priorities of the dreamer.

The term 'democracy' ought not, as the preceding chapters have tried to demonstrate, to be used as a moral yard stick. The word is not synonymous with 'the good society', and to use it to describe a political system from which 'all cause for sighing and weeping has passed away' and in which there is 'complete freedom from all social inequalities and economic insecurity' is, as Evan Durbin argues in his *Politics of Democratic Socialism*, merely to make 'democracy' synonymous with Utopia. Of course, he goes on: 'If some people choose to mean by "democracy" what other people mean by Utopia there is nothing to stop them doing so'.[1] Numbers of people have exercised this right, and so greatly added to the difficulties of meaningful discussion about democracy.

The term 'economic democracy', in particular, can have a whole gamut of differing and often ambiguous interpretations. To some, it implies the kind of egalitarianism that characterises Communist-dominated systems, in which certain causes of economic inequality such as inherited wealth, private property and a free-enterprise economy are partially eliminated and the State assumes complete control of the economy, permitting new inequalities only where these appear to the government to be in the general interest, either temporarily or permanently. To many employers in private industry in so-called capitalist countries, the term sometimes means no more than an intelligent system of labour relations, in the interests either of efficiency, or of the workers, or both. For certain sections of opinion in political parties and the trade unions, it means what has now come to be called 'participation', another vague term, which can mean no more than the organisation of information to, or of consultation of, workers regarding conditions of work and pay. It can also mean a systematic effort to interest workers in the efficiency or the profits of a firm, either by some form of profit-sharing or by financial incentives dependent on the firm's prosperity. So it can mean the cooperation of workers in the actual running of firms.

Economic democracy has also been interpreted to mean a system in which the economy is entirely run by the workers themselves with the intention of creating a complete reorganisation of society, involving the elimination of the State and of the 'wage system', by which is meant capitalism. The doctrine of Syndicalism (more correctly called revolutionary Syndicalism, since, in France, where it originated, the word *syndicalisme* means no more than trade-unionism) was an expression of the belief that a social order doing justice to the workers could never be achieved by parliamentary and constitutional means, or indeed, by political means of any kind, but only by the direct action of the workers themselves, who must take over the running of firms and industries and ultimately impose workers' control by a general strike. The democratic dialogue was to Syndicalists not merely ineffective, but the wrong method. They saw the dynamic of change as a kind of class war (though many refused to use the term), but not as orthodox Marxists see it, that is as a political operation, in which the workers are the instruments of change, under the direction of, and according to tactics determined by, political leaders. The workers are to bring about the revolution themselves in the factory or workshop and to 'supersede' the State.

Since no conceivable society could be organised through the spontaneous action of separate working units, and since a central trade-union headquarters would either become a new State or leave its country without any economic or political direction or co-ordination, the logical implication of this doctrine is anarchism. Anarcho-Syndicalism is, indeed, endemic in France, and it is comprehensible that it should have developed there, since France was, at the turn of the century when the movement became active, only partially industrialised, and had weak and

F

divided Socialist and trade-union organisations with strong local bases. Anarcho-Syndicalism was, in theory at least, an attempt to substitute action for talk, but, in practice, it merely formed the subject of more talk and more controversy. Even in France, its influence has been limited to the fringe of the Socialist and Communist Parties and the trade unions, and it has never had much influence outside France and her Latin neighbours. It has, therefore, little direct connection with democracy, since it was, and still is, essentially revolutionary. It could be seen as democratic only if one were to accept its premise that the only 'real' man is man as producer, that the economic aspect is the whole of life, and that once 'the workers' are in control, organisation and leadership will be spontaneous.

Indirectly, however, Syndicalism has influenced democratic politics, and especially Socialist politics, by encouraging belief in what Syndicalists themselves would regard as a futile, milk-and-water form of 'economic democracy', which can vary from a more militant form of trade-unionism, claiming that the mines should be run by (and presumably also for) the miners, postal services by postal workers, and so on, to schemes for greater consultation of, and participation by, workers in the running of industry. In both cases, what is now called 'industrial democracy' is conceived of as being within the democratic framework. Syndicalist theories have also directly influenced modern opponents of democratic methods, particularly in student 'radical' revolutionary organisations, both in America and in Europe, and especially in France. These movements, which are discussed in the last chapter, use much of the democratic vocabulary, describing their methods as 'more' democratic than those of existing democratic systems, and their recipe for 'economic democracy' includes the running of industries and firms by 'workers' (undefined) and the running of schools and universities by 'workers and students'. Their use of direct action, however, has no relation to democracy.

Democracy and Economic Egalitarianism

Some of the earlier anarchists and economic egalitarians did in actual fact reject society—as modern Anarcho-Syndicalists claim (not very convincingly) to do—and set up self-contained communities, sometimes in Europe, sometimes on the American continent, where they hoped to be free to live according to their principles, whether as anarchists or as economic egalitarians. Some of these communities were neither egalitarian nor democratic, others set out to be egalitarian and became authoritarian in spite of themselves. All of them broke down, sooner rather than later, and always owing to internal quarrels or schisms. Their experience is, nevertheless, relevant to the problems of modern democracy in at least two ways. It shows how easily, even in unsophisticated, small, like-minded and idealistic communities, the unrelenting search for equality can turn into a search for the kind of uniformity that results merely in equality in un-freedom. It also reveals the dependence of Utopian and doctrinaire dreamers on insulation from political and economic realities. Their doctrines appear plausible only as long as no attempt is made to put them into practice.

It is not possible within the scope of this book to give more than one or two brief illustrations.[2] The following two examples have been chosen because they are particularly relevant to the problem of reconciling liberty and equality in democracy, and because both were inspired by the principles of economic egalitarianism. The acknowledged father of revolutionary economic egalitarianism is 'Gracchus' Babeuf, whose *Conspiracy of the Equals* of 1795 arose out of his disillusionment at the failure of the French Revolution to bring equality. He believed that true equality was incompatible with the existence of private property (as did most of the egalitarians of the period). He set out, therefore, to complete the Revolution by a second and, in his view, final revolution, aimed at destroying for ever 'distinctions of rich and poor, great and small, masters and servants, governing and governed.'[3] He and his associates proposed to do this by an insurrection in which all opponents were to be exterminated (*Acte d'Insurrection*, Article 12) and all property and wealth confiscated and handed over to the State. Those who refused to comply were to have their property taxed out of existence. All inhabitants of the Republic of Equals were to live the same simple life. As the Conspirators' Manifesto put it: 'Let all the arts perish if need be, provided that we have real equality.'[4] It must be emphasised that there was nothing in the least democratic about this plan, in the normal sense of the term. On the contrary, it was frankly revolutionary and based on the wholly undemocratic assumption that the end justifies the means. Its relevance to democratic experience is that it was based on two assumptions for which evidence was lacking then, and is still lacking now, and yet that are often implicit in the plans of modern egalitarians. The first was that true equality is incompatible with the existence of private property. This assumption is no longer made by modern egalitarians in that form. Eighteenth-century egalitarians regarded all inequality as being due to the existence of private property. Twentieth-century egalitarians regard 'true' equality as incompatible with a certain number of private rights dependent on private incomes. As political dynamics, these are equivalent views. Babeuf's second assumption was that once his system had been imposed it would become generally preferred.

In reality, as is shown by the second example, that of Etienne Cabet's Icaria, nothing proved more disruptive and finally destructive of egalitarian communities than the attempt to abolish private property and to impose rigid equality. Not only did the members find equality unacceptable, even when they had initially approved of it, but they actively campaigned against it. In the best-known and most complete of the studies of a number of these egalitarian experiments, Charles Gide concluded that the hardest rule to enforce was that requiring members to give up private property, and that this caused 'unceasing strife between the communist rule and the individualist instinct'![5]

Babeuf's Republic of the Equals was never established. But Etienne Cabet's Icaria was, in 1850, and it survived for a number of years, though only at the cost of a series of schisms and fresh starts. It was formed peaceably, not by revolution, and it was based on the principle of equality, so rigidly interpreted that it required uniformity in dress, food, and everything. Cabet saw his system as the replacement of 'darkness by light, injustice by justice, domination and slavery by emancipation and freedom.'[6] It began as a Communist society in which there were 'neither rich nor poor, neither rulers nor ruled, no anxiety or worry, no crime or police, and no trials or tribunals.'[7] It did not remain in that state for long. As soon as Cabet returned to France for a time, the system broke down and order with it. Icarians acquired private property and began to feather their own nests, instead of working for the community. An opposition grew up criticising Cabet's leadership. He returned and tried to restore order by assuming dictatorial powers. An opposition party protested by striking, then resorted to violence, and eventually, the movement split into two groups. The original movement continued in existence up to the end of the century, but not without a series of feuds, splits, and fresh starts, and when the seventh colony was finally dissolved in 1898, the movement had been reduced to a mere score of members, most of whom were over 60. The egalitarian society ended with a capitalist transaction, in which the common lands were sold at a handsome profit for the owners.

It is possible to think of a number of developments in modern society in which practice has conformed equally little to the expectations of theorists. There was the belief held by supporters of the nationalisation of key sectors of the economy that nationalisation would result in better work, because workers would work harder for the State than for private employers; and there are the facts of the 'I'm alright, Jack' mentality, absenteeism, and the coincidence of rising living standards and falling trade-union discipline. There are the theories of frustration caused by economic inequalities, and the facts of trade-union strikes for the maintenance of wage differentials. There were, and still are, the theories, by no means restricted to Socialists, claiming that social services such as health and education should be a monopoly of the State in order to prevent discrimination and a sense of inequality, owing to the ability of some to pay for privileges; and there are the facts and figures of private schooling, private insurance, by no means resorted to merely by Conservatives or capitalists. The Babeuf theory, that compulsory economic equality will be accepted when it has been tried for long enough, is not borne out by accounts in modern Communist States of illicit private trading and of bribery of university-entrance examiners.

The unchallengeable fact is that no State can produce any convincing evidence of a general desire for economic equality, or of the ability of governments to come anywhere in sight of a way of obtaining it if there were such a desire, without coming up against the obstacle encountered by the Utopian egalitarians, namely, the need to choose between freedom, which in practice means diversity at the cost of some inequality, and a conception of equality which, in practice, means more uniformity than people are prepared to put up with at the cost of the freedom that they have to forego. Nevertheless, the influence of egalitarianism is still strong among political thinkers and reformers, though today, for reasons that are suggested later, its appeal is social rather than economic. It is still often Utopian. How far it owes anything directly to the egalitarian pioneers, it is hard to say, because their influence was largely superseded in Europe by that of Marx. But Marx was himself influenced by the Utopian egalitarians, in spite of his contempt for their 'unscientific' dreams and moralising, which made them, in his view, totally ineffective as revolutionary instruments. He shared, for instance, their universalism, the belief that men were much the same everywhere and that what was good for one country would, therefore, be good for all, together with the belief that it was possible to find an ideal system to remedy existing ills and that, once it had been discovered, men everywhere would come to agree on its rightness. He did not believe, however, that they could be persuaded to agree except by revolution. Nor did he believe that the revolution would come at the same time in all countries. He also shared their assumption (which was that of most eighteenth-century reformers) that society's political and economic ills were attributable to the way in which it was organised, and in particular to the economic environment and the existence of private property. His objective, like theirs, was an egalitarian society, though he saw equality in terms of classlessness. He was also just as selective in his use of 'the facts of history' to support his comprehensive 'scientific' explanation of the social process as any Utopian had ever been in his use of 'the facts' of human psychology to justify egalitarianism.

Whether directly or as transmuted by Marx, egalitarian assumptions and theorising have certainly helped to increase the predilection in European political thought, and especially in Socialist and Communist thought, for doctrinal controversy and theoretical systematising. In France, where they originated, they have become part of the permanent background of left-wing thought. In Germany, Italy and France, the fact that Socialist Parties have all, in one way or another, had to find a *modus vivendi* with large Communist Parties has condemned them to prolonged periods in opposition, and so increased the scope for sterile doctrinal quarrels, while depriving parties of the stimulus to realism provided by the responsibilities of governmental office. In France and Italy, where the Communist Party has been strongest, the result has been a continuous proliferation of dissident left-wing parties, in differing degrees, Social-Democrat, Egalitarian, and Marxist or Anarchist. Directly or indirectly, then, egalitarian theorists and the class theories of Marx have helped to produce a left-wing political climate in some European countries very different from that of democratic Socialism in Britain and the Scandinavian countries, and so have helped to invalidate the original Marxist conception of 'the workers' as being essentially similar whatever their nationality.

Industrial Democracy and 'Participation'

Among ideas derived from theories of 'economic democracy', but capable of practical application within the general framework of democratic systems, what is called industrial democracy has played a small but not negligible part, and 'participation' may play a part in the future. In its early British form of Guild Socialism, associated in the years before the first world war with the Fabian Socialist economist, G. D. H. Cole, it still had elements of Utopianism about it. It was influenced by the theories of Ruskin and William Morris, and was a movement inspired by middle-class intellectuals that never won very much support among the trade unions. Indeed, G. D. H. Cole himself, later recognised that it was 'a politically-minded person's Utopia' and admitted that he had found no agreement, either in the Labour Party or in the Trades Union Congress, on how the principles of industrial democracy could be applied, but that, on the contrary, he had found 'a deep distrust of the workers' power to run industry on self-governing lines or of their preparedness to do this in the common interest rather than in their own.'[8]

Nevertheless, though Guild Socialism was short-lived and was a specifically Socialist idea, its basic principle of workers' participation, though falling short of control, has remained a preoccupation in some circles of the Labour Party[9], and the idea of 'participation', including plans for profit-sharing, has also attracted support within the Liberal Party. In France, 'participation' became official governmental policy under the Gaullist regime, and a law was passed in 1967, after some two years of passionate argument and recrimination, providing for a modest amount of profit-sharing in some of the larger firms. It was criticised both on technical grounds and on grounds of inequality

—some sections of workers being eligible for much greater amounts than other, and some being likely to receive nothing. The trade unions were strongly opposed to the whole scheme and even organised protest strikes against it. After the events of May and June, 1968, 'participation' was extended to the running of universities and secondary schools, in the form of student representation on various joint committees concerned with the administration, and the government announced that it would be extended in industry to allow workers to participate in the profits of firms.

So far, 'participation' remains in an introductory phase, with little on which to judge its worth beyond statements of the principle and the tentative constitution of committees with limited functions. But the French experiment, nevertheless, illustrates clearly the basic difficulties that supporters of the principle have always encountered when it came to putting it into practice. The first is that, both among workers and employers, there are strong elements of resistance to the whole idea. Employers feel that it is their job to run industry. Numbers of workers, as G. D. H. Cole realised, share this view, and in any case do not want to undertake the responsibility, or give their time to administrative tasks. And the trade unions, organised to negotiate with employers on behalf of their members, do not want to have their loyalties confused by becoming, in however minor a form, co-bosses. Marxist trade unions have, of course, far stronger objections. However much they are, in practice, prepared to reach reasonable understandings with the employers, they remain in theory advocates of the class war, and cannot, therefore, accept a system in which their rank and file would not clearly see them as being on the opposite side from the employers.

'Participation' in the universities, whether in France or in Britain, is likely to run into far more complex difficulties that cannot be discussed within the scope of this book, except, perhaps, for the reminder that, as M. Pompidou put it, 'Youth is not a state of being, but a transition, and a rapid one at that. Before there is time to understand one generation, the next is already there.'[10] In any case, 'participation' in schools and universities can hardly be considered as constituting 'economic' democracy. If it belongs anywhere, it is to the field of 'social' democracy. Indeed, the popularity of the idea of 'participation' in general is symptomatic of the change of focus of political re-formers in the mid-twentieth century.

'*Social*' Democracy

This change of focus has been the result of two factors in particular. The first is the changing nature of national economies and of economic relations from the 1950s onwards. On the one hand, there has been the generalisation of social security, full employment, and continuing redistribution of incomes. Demo-cratic freedom has, therefore, come to be looked on less as freedom *from* want and as freedom *to* work, and more as freedom *in* work and freedom to enjoy facilities created by a higher standard of living. Conditions of leisure, for instance, have become important as well as the level of income and the conditions of work. On the other hand, the evolution of the economic system itself has made many of the older attitudes to 'economic' democracy inapplicable. The existence of large public sectors, working alongside private industry (and often offering their workers inferior conditions and pay), the growth of co-operation between employers and trade unions and be-tween government (of whatever political complexion) and trade unions, the spread of government planning and the increasing association of government and trade-union representatives with-in this framework—all these have made the traditional pre-occupations of economic egalitarians appear increasingly irrele-vant. The status of the worker demonstrably no longer depends on whether the 'commanding heights of the economy', or in-deed any other heights, are publicly or privately owned. What has come to be regarded as more important is 'the degree to which management is autocratic or democratic, the extent of joint consultation and participation, and the freedom of the worker to strike or leave his job.'[11]

The emphasis of contemporary democratic thought is becom-ing now predominantly social, and this applies to liberal demo-crats as well as to Socialists, because no party in developed Western European countries today expects the capitalist system to collapse in the near future, or to be replaced in any dramatic or sudden way by something called Socialism. The welfare State is neither capitalist nor Socialist. The very meaning of Socialism has become unclear to many Socialists themselves.

The authors of a Socialist attempt in 1956 to rethink Socialist ethics applied to the sphere of economic organisation, concluded that ' ... socialists are now divided and confused. The very success of their achievements seems to threaten the ground beneath their feet. Any belief that the workers could hope for nothing, except increasing misery, under capitalism has been destroyed with a completeness beyond argument.'[12]

The ground beneath the feet of other parties is no less unsure. There is no longer any clear-cut distinction between what used to be regarded as capitalist or Socialist methods in industry. And in the changed economic climate, the traditional appeal of 'economic' democracy has become, if not meaningless, ineffective as a political dynamic. All parties are reformists, all are limited in their possibilities of action by economic and international circumstances over which individual nations have little control. All are concerned to improve the quality of social life by finding ways of preventing the individual from being submerged in an economic and political machine whose increasing size and complexity seem to reduce him more and more to the status of a cypher—a mere statistic. The need to increase the selectivity of the social services, in order to help the specially handicapped—the old, the ill, the children of broken homes, the feckless and incompetent parents, criminals, delinquents, the psychologically abnormal and so on, the need to get rid of 'the division of society into classes', and the 'extravagant differences in income that are a barrier to a common mode of life'[13]— these are the policies of all democratic parties.

But what is the political dynamic? The answer to that question is provided by the second factor, the changing roles in political life of economists and sociologists. It is difficult to decide the extent to which this change is a cause or an effect of the changes in the economic climate. But what has happened is that the increasing focus of political parties on social welfare and the concern of sociologists with the analysis of class structures have combined to make what is called 'social' democracy 'the desire for an equal and classless society'—the most distinctive political objective of the late 1960s. 'Participation' is one expression of 'social' democracy. Another is the preoccupation with social equality and with ways of attaining it through the levelling influences of social services, and above all, through a unified and increasingly uniform national educational system.

In his book, *The Future of Socialism,* Mr Anthony Crosland describes this objective of 'social equality and the "classless society"' as a 'distinctive socialist ideal'.[14] It would be hard to substantiate this, and harder by reference to what parties do than to what they say. Over the 15 years between 1955 and 1970, British Conservative and Labour policies in the fields of social security, health and education policies, and of wages and prices policies, have not differed significantly enough to provide any clear-cut line between them insofar as social levelling is concerned. The main reason may be that neither party has had significant freedom to manoeuvre owing to the priorities imposed by the economic circumstances. But the Liberal Party too, which has had no need to be unduly preoccupied with electoral considerations, shows exactly similar preoccupations with social policies. In France, where the non-Communist opposition was hopelessly divided and ineffective following the events of 1968, the official Gaullist policy of educational reform and industrial as well as educational 'participation' was not really opposed by any specific section of political opinion. In Germany, it was difficult to understand exactly where Socialist and non-Socialist partners in the governmental coalition of 1966 to 1969 parted company. More and more, the real dividing line seems to be, not between democratic parties, but, within them, and the real divisions seem to be increasingly on the issue of the desirability or the credibility of objectives of social equality and a classless society.

These conceptions of 'social democracy' are open to essentially the same objections as those raised by the objective of 'economic' egalitarianism, namely doubts as to whether 'social', any more than 'economic' equality can possibly be achieved by political means, and as to whether the majority of citizens in any country really share the enthusiasm of sociologists and educational reformers for the idea of equality. Egalitarians have never succeeded in determining exactly where to draw the line between equality and uniformity or in discovering how to ensure, therefore, that, in the name of equality, the liberty of individuals to develop to the full their unique personalities will not be curtailed. Nor have they ever succeeded in explaining how they are to recognise the precise point at which all *unnatural* equalities, such as wealth, status, educational and social opportunity, will have been eliminated, leaving only the *natural* inequalities that cannot be eliminated by political action. Nor, as was said in the preceding chapter, is there any convincing evidence that the majority of individuals want equality or have ever wanted it. As the example of numbers of egalitarian communities has shown, attempts to make equality the rule have always failed. Evidence of the desire of people to be different —to be unequal—abounds in all societies, from the desire for office, distinctions, status, rank, decorations, and so on, to the simple desire to look different, or as different as fashion, conventions and habits allow.

In one way, an unrelenting pursuit of social equality may prove more likely than the pursuit of economic equality to destroy democracy itself. For once egalitarians go beyond the attempt to eliminate real economic inequalities and seek to eliminate possible or likely causes of feelings of inferiority, they are setting out on a road that seems likely to be endless. The more inequalities they remove, the more potential inequalities they will discover. In a Fabian pamphlet, published in 1964, the author first demands action 'to ensure that the major public schools cease to perform their present function of perpetuating the class structure'.[15] But a few pages later, he notes that a child's class background, his family background, and even the size of his family, can all have an adverse effect on his IQ and his educational attainment. It would be possible to go on enumerating indefinitely the number of factors that _could_ have such an adverse effect. And among them would be many that no political system could begin to do anything about. But in the process of chopping away at one real or imagined privilege after another, the egalitarians could also eliminate much of the individual freedom that is an even more essential objective of democracy.

The problem of how to reconcile liberty and equality is a very old one, and is probably insoluble. The experience of the past does suggest, however, that to make either economic or social equality an overriding priority is certainly not going to make it any easier to deal with. The practice of governments has been in the main pragmatic, that is, to seek to remedy recognised grievances or to eliminate as far as possible clearly perceptible inequalities, in other words, it has been based on the attempt to level up or level down in ways that would reduce differences of social and educational opportunity, whether based on physical, economic or social disadvantages. The reduction of differences between classes has followed as a by-product, and will probably continue to do this, not merely because the whole notion of 'class' is subjective, vague, and is continually changing in ways that governments can do little or nothing to influence directly, but also because governments can rarely afford the luxury of policies that are not compromises between many different and conflicting ideas and interests.

Part II

Some Problems of Democratic Practice

6

Constitutions

As Constitutions are baptismal certificates to newly independent nations, so are they marriage contracts for federations.

William G. Andrews, Constitutions and Constitutionalism

Against mass hysteria no plausible constitutional safeguard has yet been proposed.

R. Wollheim, Democracy, Journal of the
History of Ideas, April 1958

Constitutional Variety

The usual starting point for any discussion of democratic institutions is the constitution, that is, the general framework which determines the powers of, and the basic relationships between, the different organs of government in a given country. For constitutions have been bound up with the growth of modern democracy, having been generally regarded for nearly two centuries as providing essential safeguards against the exercise of arbitrary power. Unfortunately for those who want a simple recipe for democracy, there is no possible general blueprint for a democratic constitution. There are wide variations between different types of constitution, and between different constitutions of the same type. They may be written or unwritten, monarchical or republican, parliamentary or presidential, unitary or federal, difficult to amend or flexible, long and complicated or short and straightforward. The most flexible constitution imaginable is that of Great Britain, where the procedure for revision is simply the ordinary legislative procedure. A Bill to regulate the opening hours of public houses and one to amend the succession to the throne are passed or rejected in exactly the same way. There is indeed no recognised way of distinguishing 'constitutional' from any other legislative enactments, since there is no single document in existence called the British Constitution, which brings together the enactments that other countries describe as constitutional. In Britain, the terms 'constitutional' and 'unconstitutional' are really no more than value judgements, expressing the speaker's assessment of their basic importance. Political scientists and lawyers do, of course, make the distinction in numerous textbooks, but any government is free to ignore them.[1]

Great Britain is, however, for reasons discussed later, an exception. Almost all civilised countries today, whether democratic or not, have written constitutions, and it is possible to make a certain number of generalisations about them, though, given the enormous variations, these are not always very illuminating. Since a constitution supplies 'the collection of legal rules and non-legal rules which govern the government',[2] their content must by definition deal with the composition, duties and relations with each other of the organs of government—executive, legislative and judicial—together with some statements concerning the ways in which their functions are to be carried out. Few constitutions limit themselves to this, though the United States Constitution, as it existed when it came into force in 1789, consisted of only seven articles, of which five dealt respectively with the legislature, the executive, the judiciary, the rights retained by the 13 member-States and the methods of constitutional revision. The Constitution of the Third French Republic consisted merely of three separate laws dealing with the election of the President, his relations with the Government and the two legislative Chambers and the composition of the second Chamber, the Senate.

Most democratic systems, however, regard the constitution as being much more than a businesslike book of rules. It is also intended to be something that informs and reassures the citizen as to his place in the State, that outlines individuals rights and sometimes individual obligations. In 1791, the United States Constitution added ten amendments to the original document, of which nine deal with the rights and liberties of the individual citizen and the tenth with the collective rights of each of the constituent States. The first French constitution, which was monarchical, and four of the five French Republican constitutions, together with two important Republican constitutions that were drawn up but never came into force, all include statements of the rights of the citizen, largely reproducing the original Declaration of the Rights of Man and the Citizen published in 1789. The Basic Law of the Federal Republic of Germany begins with a section of 19 articles dealing with the basic rights of citizens, that of Mexico with a section on individual guarantees. Those of India and Japan, like the Communist constitutions of the U.S.S.R., Yugoslavia and China, all include sections dealing with the duties as well as the rights of citizens.

It might be assumed that, since the aim of a constitution is to provide a framework of rules, on the basis of which a stable code of political behaviour can be built up, one of the general characteristics of constitutions would be their longevity, even in countries with traditions of short-lived governments. If longevity were to be one of the tests of a good constitution, however, relatively few would pass it. Most of the newly independent African States, all of which drew up constitutions on acceding to independence, had begun to revise them almost before the ink was dry. Within a few years, many had already been overthrown and replaced by some form of emergency or military rule, or both. Some show no sign of returning to normal constitutional rule in the foreseeable future. In Europe, too, there has been considerable constitutional instability. Federal Germany's present constitution, called the Basic Law, dates only from 1949, the previous one (the Weimar Constitution of 1919) having been overthrown by Hitler. Italy's constitution of 1948 followed the years of Fascist rule that replaced the former democratic constitution in 1926. The democratic constitutions of the Netherlands, Belgium and the Scandinavian countries have survived for much longer periods, but not without a number of radical revisions. France, however, holds what must be a world record for constitutional change and experiment. Since 1789, she has had at least 13 written constitutions and at least two extensive constitutional revisions that were only formally distinct from a change of régime. She has had three monarchical constitutions (1791, 1814, 1830), two dictatorial (the year VIII and the year X), three imperial (the year XII, the *acte additionnel* of 1815 and 1852), and five Republican (1795, 1848, 1875, 1946, 1958). She also had four constitutions which, though written, never came into force (the two Republican constitutions of 1793, the Senatorial constitution of 1814 and the first Republican constitution of 1946), and three provisional régimes based on no written document (1848, 1870 and 1940).

No country has provided political scientists with such a rich field of constitutional experiments. This helps to explain, and if necessary to justify, the frequency with which problems of constitutional theory and practice discussed in these pages are illustrated by examples taken from French constitutional experience.

Constitutional Vagueness

One of the major difficulties in attempting to assess the content of constitutions is the impossibility of knowing what promises or 'guarantees' in articles dealing with the rights and duties of citizens are really worth, and what is actually meant by articles attributing functions to certain governmental organs or personalities without any provisions indicating how they are to be carried out, if indeed they *can* be carried out. What they mean in practice depends on how they are interpreted by governments in different countries, and on how far citizens are vigilant enough to prevent their governments from either failing to enforce them, or from adopting abusive interpretations. Rights and duties are invariably stated in brief and general terms, and indeed it is difficult to see how a constitution can do more than that. It should not try to perform the same function as a law. Difficulties arise, however, if the necessary legislation to give meaning to general constitutional principles is not passed. One example of such difficulties has arisen in relation to Article 5 of the Constitution of the Fifth French Republic. Here, what is in question is the nature of the duty of the President of the Republic, who is made responsible for ensuring 'respect for the Constitution, the regular functioning of the public authorities and the continuity of the State'. Neither this nor any other article of the constitution gives any guidance on how he is to perform this duty or on who is to judge whether he is performing it satisfactorily. Nor has any legislation dealt with the problem. In practice the article was interpreted by President de Gaulle as giving him the sole right both to decide how best to carry out these duties and to judge his own performance. This interpretation was generally accepted—and not only by the President's supporters.

Another article of the same constitution recognises the right of citizens to form parties, whose freedom of action is to be unrestricted provided that they respect 'the principles of national sovereignty and of democracy', (Article 4). This article has been widely interpreted by political scientists as meaning that France could not constitutionally become a one-party State and that the Communist Party could constitutionally be banned only if it failed to fulfil these conditions. But who is to be the judge and on what criteria is not stated either in the constitution or anywhere else. In Article 21 of the Basic Law of the German Federal Republic, the right to form parties is accompanied by conditions formulated in strikingly similar terms, but with the difference that, in Germany, the Federal Constitutional Court is entrusted with the task of deciding whether the conditions have been complied with. It is difficult to believe that German and French Communists have significantly different attitudes to the principles of national sovereignty and democracy. Yet Germany has banned the Communist Party and France has not.[3]

In some cases, vagueness is intentional. Constitutions are made by politicians who are bound by their loyalty to their own party doctrines and attitudes, and sometimes in addition by the requirements of coalition governments. Those who were responsible for the drawing up of the 1946 French Constitution could not have avoided, even if they had wanted to, including the right to strike among the enumeration of the rights of the citizen, since the National Assembly had a strong left-wing majority. The majority in the country was less sympathetic to the left-wing views, as was made clear when the referendum on the first draft of the constitution resulted in its rejection. The political disadvantages from the point of view of any government of an unrestricted right to strike are obvious. The compromise adopted was the inclusion in the constitution of the principle of the right to strike, accompanied by certain safeguards. One was the recognition of the right 'within the framework of the laws regulating it'. The other was the relegation of all these vaguely phrased individual rights, including the right to strike, to the Preamble instead of including them in the body of the constitution, as had been done in the first draft. The law regulating the exercise of the right to strike was not voted until 1963 (and even then dealt with it only partially). The extent to which the content of the Preamble was to be regarded as having the same weight as articles of the constitution remained a matter of juridical argument, and in consequence, the legal and constitutional position of strikers was never wholly clear.

There is a similar lack of precision in the constitutional right affirmed after the Civil War by the fifteenth amendment to the American Constitution. Section 1 states that the right to vote 'cannot be denied or abridged by the United States or by any State on account of race, colour or previous condition of servitude'. Section 2 states that Congress has power to enforce this by 'appropriate legislation'. As has been mentioned earlier, a number of States used this power to defeat the intentions of Section 1, by introducing restrictive electoral qualifications, theoretically applicable to all, but in practice applied almost exclusively to Negroes.

In defence of such vagueness, which many people will regard simply as hypocrisy, it is necessary to remember that the primary function of a democratic constitution is not to *impose* moral standards of behaviour on an unwilling electorate, but to prescribe standards that the majority is willing to accept. To go too far ahead of opinion is to risk, therefore, either failing to get agreement on a constitution or seeing unpopular clauses flouted, and thus discrediting the constitution itself in the process. An example of this is provided by the history of Prohibition in the United States. It is arguable whether such a matter should properly be included in a constitution at all. That this was done was doubtless in the hope that more respect would be accorded to a constitutional measure than to one that had merely legal status. There was also the practical advantage that a constitutional amendment coerced recalcitrant member-States of the Federation and would be more difficult to amend than an ordinary law. But after 13 years, Prohibition had to be replaced by another constitutional amendment, because the constitutional obligation had been systematically and increasingly evaded, and the constitution thereby discredited. Faced with a political controversy on the principle of obligatory voting, the authors of the 1948 Italian Constitution compromised, by affirming (Article 48) that 'the exercise of the vote is a civic duty', leaving it open to supporters of obligatory voting to press for legislative sanctions against non-voters, and to opponents to resist this.

It is, in fact, very difficult to draw the line between the kind of ambiguity or vagueness that has just been discussed and deliberate hypocrisy, which is not unknown in constitutions.

Nations, like political parties, sometimes feel obliged to proclaim principles that they have no real intention of translating into practice, just as churchgoers often feel obliged to make a periodic renunciation of sin, without any intention of mending their ways forthwith, and adulterers are often as ready as anyone to pay tribute to the institution of marriage. Examples of this characteristic can be found in the constitutions of democratic as well as non-democratic States. For instance, the French Constitutions of 1946 and 1958[4] both state that 'the law guarantees to women equal rights with men in all fields'. If this was meant as a statement of fact, it was untrue when it was written; if it was meant as a statement of future obligation, the obligation is still unfulfilled. The Soviet Constitution accords to every Union Republic the right to secede from the U.S.S.R. (Article 17), and recognises both freedom of speech and of the press (Article 125). Ukrainians who might be tempted to take the first at its face value can have no illusions as to what would happen to them in the light of what happened to Hungary and Czechoslovakia—both of them, it must be remembered, independent nations with their own constitutions—when they tried to move only one or two steps away from strict obedience to a Soviet-dictated political line. And there have been many writers before Daniel and Sinyavsky who have had ample time in Soviet prisons to reflect on the precise value to be attached to Article 125.

The difficulties that can arise from this kind of imprecision are obvious, the advantages sometimes less so. If constitutional principles on which there is, or is likely to be, political controversy are too clearly and restrictively defined, they can make a constitution into a straitjacket. A successful constitution is built to last and must, therefore, be capable of adaptation and amendment on specific points, while retaining its essential authority. The only way to get out of a straitjacket is to break out. Among many difficulties of constitution-makers, there is, on the one hand, that of recognising where to draw the line between a formulation that is too precise to be applicable and one that is too vague to be meaningful, and, on the other, that of obtaining the necessary political support to make what is desirable also politically possible.

Constitutions and Political Necessities

Sometimes the only possible solution is to leave certain provisions out altogether. Both the inclusion and the omission of constitutional provisions are at times dictated by the inevitable influence on constitution-makers of current political issues. These are not always lasting, and may soon become constitutionally irrelevant, if indeed they were ever theoretically relevant. But in a democratic system, it is public opinion that, in the last resort, determines what is or is not constitutionally relevant, and what governments can ignore only at their peril. There is, thus, no criterion, other than that of political necessity, for the inclusion or omission of a number of provisions in constitutions. Electoral rules, for instance, are sometimes included and sometimes omitted, and for differing reasons. In federal States, they are often regarded as being, at least partially, outside the sphere of federal government. In the United States, as has been said, the determination of electoral qualifications is left to the member-States.[5] In the German Federal Republic, federal elections are governed by Federal law and the *Länder* have their own electoral systems (subject to some degree of control). The constitution merely states that: 'All State authority emanates from the people. It is exercised by the people by means of elections and voting and by separate legislative, executive and judicial organs' (Article 20). The Soviet Constitution does include some electoral rules (Article 34, 35, 134–42), though the system of election to local Soviets is left to be determined by the Union Republics (Article 96).

In France, which has a unitary system, the earlier constitutions did include electoral rules (1791, 1795 and 1848), but the Third, Fourth and Fifth Republican constitutions did not. By then, electoral systems had become one of the most persistently divisive political issues and so no lasting agreement on them was possible. It is one thing to agree on an electoral law, if it can be regarded as temporary and easily changeable with a change of government. It is quite another to give constitutional status to an electoral system, which means deliberately seeking to make it either permanent or changeable only with some difficulty. Governments do not want changes in the electoral system to risk creating a constitutional crisis.

Electoral systems are, of course, not the only example of the conflict between political necessity and constitutional theory. Among other examples of matters included in constitutions for predominantly political reasons there can be quoted, for instance, the third, eighteenth and twenty-first amendments to the United States Constitution. The first of these forbids the quartering of soldiers in any house in time of peace without the consent of the owner, and requires this to be done, even in time of war, only in a manner prescribed by law. The second imposes and the third repeals Prohibition. The fact that the constitution of the German Federal Republic is entitled only 'Basic Law', and specifically states that it is intended to last only until 'a constitution adopted by a free decision of the German people comes into force' (Article 146) clearly indicates the desire to reassure German opinion regarding the government's continued loyalty to the policy of German reunification. Communist governments are anxious to emphasise that their constitutions are ushering in a new political era, and so devote a number of articles to the expression of ideological principles, proclaiming the overthrow of capitalism and the vesting of all power in workers and peasants (Articles 1–12 of the Soviet Constitution, and articles 1 and 6–26 of the Yugoslav Constitution, for instance).

Some subjects are omitted from constitutions, on the other hand, because they were not political issues at the time, and so there was no pressure to have them included. Among such subjects are many that can become acutely controversial, as for instance, questions of parliamentary procedure or questions concerning the position of the armed forces, the regulation of the educational system, the problem of provision for religious education in schools, the nature of the restrictions that should be imposed on the right of private property. All of these have been hotly debated during the drawing up of French constitutions, and the decision whether to include them, and if they are included, the precise formulation of the provisions, have varied considerably from one constitution to another.

Is Your Constitution Really Necessary?

If what is regarded as constitutional can vary so much from one period and one country to another, if democratic as well as non-democratic constitutions can so often be overthrown or

radically revised, if their provisions can be ignored or interpreted in different ways, why is there near-unanimity outside
Britain on the need for a written constitution? One answer
could be that rational justification for political acts is not necessary, that in politics as in everything else there are conventions
and fashions, and that politics in all countries include a fairly
high percentage of pious hopes, hypocrisy, and declarations of
good intentions, and that all that really matters in a democracy
is whether people *want* a constitution. If they do, then a democratic system must provide one. This is very far from a complete answer.

The real case for constitutions is that, provided the conditions
necessary for constitutional government are present—and in
most African countries, and some European countries too,
they are not—they can play a useful political role. By providing
an agreed framework for political institutions (and agreement
on the framework is, of course, one of the essential conditions
for success), a constitution can help to narrow the field of political
controversy and so help to encourage the growth of political
stability. By singling out certain institutions and issues as having
fundamental importance for the citizens as a whole, it gives
special weight to them and so can help to create a psychological
atmosphere in which most people will think twice before changing them. Even if some rights and duties enumerated are not
enforced, a solemn declaration of their importance and of the
State's recognition of this can help to arouse public interest in
them, to create respect for them, and to strengthen moral and
political pressure for their recognition in practice as well as in
theory. They can become moral criteria by which governments
and parties are judged. That this does happen is indicated by the
greater unwillingness of political parties to have certain controversial issues 'constitutionalised',[6] than to have them regulated
by law. It is indicated too, by the importance attached in the
minds of so many people to the United Nations Declaration
of Human Rights of 1948. For this document cannot claim
to have more than moral authority, since the United Nations
has no machinery by which signatories can be compelled to
fulfil their obligations.

One way in which nations often try to ensure that a constitution acquires the degree of moral authority conferred by its
general acceptance over a long period of time is by deliberately

making the amending process difficult. It is doubtful whether this is a very effective method, in view of the fact that one of the assumptions of democracy is precisely that political circumstances are perpetually changing and that institutions must keep pace with changing needs. It can be argued that a constitution is more likely to survive if it is flexible rather than rigid, that the more it can bend, the less likely it is to break.

This is no doubt true, once it has become established in a political climate of settled government in which there is widespread respect for legality and the rule of law. But most constitutions in the modern world are born in unsettled periods and intended to be instruments that will help to create the essential political stability. In these circumstances, the more a country needs the benefits of constitutional government, the less likely it is to obtain them. If, as so often happens, the constitution seeks, not to record the maximum discoverable area of agreement, but to consolidate the political victory of some political elements over others, then it is likely to be from the start an additional divisive factor, instead of a force making for unity. Where a constitution becomes part of the political battle instead of being above it, neither side will have the necessary confidence in the other not to use the constitution as an additional political weapon.

This has only too often been the situation in France, during her long history of constitutional change. After the 1939-45 war, the restoration of the constitution of the Third Republic was rejected by a majority of Frenchmen for political rather than for constitutional reasons. Revision of one or two contested articles could have made it a workable instrument for any combination of political parties, and it had the additional advantage of having been in operation for almost three-quarters of a century. Instead, because it was too much associated in people's minds with the parties held to have been responsible for France's military defeat in 1940, the majority preferred a fresh start. The parties in power wanted a constitutional fresh start for other reasons as well. They wanted a constitution expressing more of their own left-wing principles. But they were not even agreed among themselves on what should replace the previous constitution, and so the result was a year of constitutional bickering, followed by eleven and half years during most of which the constitution was itself a subject of political controversy.

That of 1958, which followed General de Gaulle's return to power, represented, to some extent, the expression of the political victory of forces that had disliked the 1946 constitution from the start. The tables were therefore turned and, for the first seven years of the régime, the left-wing opposition parties, though still politically divided, were at least agreed that when they returned to power the constitution must once again be changed.

In the case of newly independent African and Asian countries, the difficulties of establishing stable constitutional government are infinitely greater. Their peoples have had no political experience except under conditions of colonial rule, and they have not yet built up the essential infra-structure of a developed democratic system—regular party machines, political traditions, an administration of trained civil servants free from corruption. They also have to wrestle with a whole series of problems that in Western democracies are either non-existent, such as tribalism, or much less serious, such as economic under-development, or economic non-viability without massive external aid. Even in the most favourable circumstances, independence in African countries was bound to be followed by a long period of political instability, during which political disturbances were only too likely to end in constitutional breakdown. In many of them, the attempt to develop a democratic system was soon abandoned and replaced by one-party rule.

Where States have been formed from heterogeneous elements, with strong regional, racial, tribal, or religious differences, the difficulties of constitutional democratic government are increased by those inherent in a federal constitution, which alone can adequately safeguard minority interests of this kind. The inevitable rigidities of a federal system have been demonstrated in the breakdown of the Mali, Guinea, Ghana, and Central African Federations, and in the war between the breakaway State of Biafra and the Nigerian Federation.

In the United States, Switzerland, Australia and Canada, federal constitutions have proved workable, but in these countries, not only were populations more homogeneous than, say, those of India and Africa, but there had also been considerable experience of democratic forms of government before they acquired their present constitutional status. Up to now, the two essential conditions of successful constitutional government have been present in most of these countries, namely, a long experience of settled democratic institutions, together with the existence of a constitutional consensus. Political quarrels have thus not developed into constitutional crises. Whether Canada can resist indefinitely the threat to constitutional consensus posed by the growing assertiveness of the French-speaking provinces is, however, in some doubt. And the desire of the white population to impose *apartheid* in South Africa has given rise to one long constitutional struggle ending in constitutional amendment. In the others, where no such strains were present, the federal system has undoubtedly acted as a brake on political change. To the former Australian Prime Minister, Mr Menzies, that was one of its advantages. 'It is more difficult for Socialists to have their way in a federal country', he said in 1948, 'than in a unitary country like Britain'.' This may be all right as long as Socialists are not likely to be in power. But once they are, if the constitution hampers them in applying a programme accepted by the majority of electors in democratic elections, then there is a threat to the consensus that should prevent the constitution from becoming a subject of political controversy.

Both Australia and Switzerland have mitigated the rigidity of the amending process of their federal constitutions by providing for a referendum in certain circumstances, though referenda have generally in practice proved to have a conservative influence. The United States has the most rigid of all federal constitutions. In the first place, the amending process is difficult, for amendment requires a majority for the proposal in three-quarters of the States. Since these have equal status in spite of tremendous differences in their populations, this requirement can give a power of veto to a small minority. In the second place, the division of power between the executive, the legislature and the judiciary is such that each acts as a check on the others, thus creating a permanent risk of political deadlock.

Though such deadlock does happen at times, particularly during years when the President heads a party which is in a minority in the Congress, in practice, a number of ways have been found of circumventing these obstacles, the most important of which is the re-interpretation by the Supreme Court of certain articles of the constitution. For instance, it would never have been possible to introduce the policy of racial integration in American schools and universities by means of the amending process laid down in the constitution because the Southern States could easily have prevented it from being adopted. What happened, as everybody knows, was that the Supreme Court in 1954 re-interpreted the relevant article of the constitution, thus amending the constitution in practice, while leaving the actual wording intact. An earlier interpretation had permitted the States to provide separate schools and universities for white and Negro populations. The new interpretation made this unconstitutional. Even so, it has taken years, and a number of interventions by the federal authorities, to enforce even partial compliance with this ruling.

This indirect constitutional amendment by re-interpretation enables a rigid constitution to be more responsive to changing opinions. There also grow up in all constitutional systems a number of unwritten conventions which give much greater elasticity to the relations between the different organs of government, and so allow changes of opinion to be reflected in institutions without involving the difficulties of direct constitutional amendment. Thus, for years, it was generally understood that an American President ought not to stand for a third term of office, though nothing in the constitution forbade him to do so. This unwritten rule was broken for the first time in 1940 and 1944, when President Roosevelt stood and was elected for a third and then a fourth term. The circumstances were exceptional, in that this was during the war. The unwritten rule was, nevertheless, made a constitutional obligation in 1951 by the twenty-second amendment.

Unofficial legislative and executive contacts have often helped to prevent the development of serious political deadlocks. One of the most important American conventions has been the general acceptance of the right of the President to make 'executive agreements' with foreign powers, applicable without waiting for the ratification by the Senate, which in the case of treaties is required by the constitution. If these and many other devices have helped the American constitution to survive in the conditions of the twentieth century, this has, however, been at the price of piling up a vast mass of complicated legal machinery that has led students of the American constitution to describe it as having created a lawyer's paradise.

Though the British constitution is so flexible that the whole parliamentary system could, in theory, be abolished by ordinary legislation, in practice, it has been no more subject than has the American constitution to hasty or irresponsible revision. One reason for this is the fact that the major political battles which so often involve constitutional instability were fought out so many years ago that victors and vanquished have long since ceased to regard them as live political issues. The British constitution grew up piecemeal over the centuries, its provisions being expressed in a number of statutory laws, and in common, or customary, law, continuously subject to re-interpretation by successive judicial decisions, as well as in unwritten conventions accepted by government and opposition alike, and changed as and when necessary by general—sometimes tacit —agreement. By the time that written constitutions became fashionable from the end of the eighteenth century onwards, Magna Carta, the Bill of Rights, Habeas Corpus, the Act of Settlement, the Union with Scotland, religious toleration, the fundamental rights and liberties of the citizen—all these were already accepted as part of the existing political system (though equality between the holders of different religious beliefs was not yet complete). Britain already had a long experience of parliamentary government, and there was general confidence in the capacity of Parliament to make changes as and when they became necessary. There has, therefore, been no point of history at which the British have felt the need for a written constitution, except during the Commonwealth, which turned out to be merely an interlude. The British system has had its political crises, some of them on constitutional issues, notably on the question of the House of Lords. But these have not since 1688 involved any real threat to the régime. Whether this will continue to be true in the future, nobody can say.

What Constitutions Cannot Do

Nothing indeed can guarantee that conditions that have permitted successful constitutional government will be permanent. However well a country's constitution works, however wise its politicians are, there are limits to what ought to be expected of any constitution. Mention has already been made of the differences between theory and practice. To some extent these are, and must be, inherent and inescapable. For if a constitution is to have real political influence, its general principles must be expressed in a form that is comprehensible to the average citizen. This implies that it must be capable of translation into relatively simple concepts embodied in a fairly short document. No less than political speeches and declarations of political parties it will have to over-simplify issues. Implementing legislation, on the other hand, will have to be detailed and complex in order to take into account the practical difficulties and unforeseen problems that always crop up when general principles are applied to special cases.

This necessary area of discretion undoubtedly provides a built-in opportunity for governments to water down or evade in practice some of the obligations accepted in principle. No political system, however, can function without some such safety valve, because the decisions as to *how* and *when* constitutional provisions can be applied must be based on the political circumstances in the country in question. It is really misleading to speak of a constitution as 'guaranteeing' anything. This is a word regularly used in constitutional vocabulary, partly to encourage respect for constitutional provisions, partly because, in a stable constitutional system, governments will seek as far as is politically possible to transform them into guarantees by using the machinery of the State—political, legal and, if necessary, military—to compel respect for the laws which define precisely what constitutional principles are to be understood to mean. But it is the implementing legislation, not the formulation of the principle, that constitutes the real guarantee. And the extent to which governments are able to give such guarantees must be determined, in a democratic system, by their estimate of the extent to which they will be supported by the legislatures on which they depend, directly or indirectly, for their survival, and by public opinion, which, in the last resort, determines the fate of both governments and legislature.

In so far as a constitution guarantees anything, then, it does so as the reflection and expression of political will, and so must be capable of continuous adaptation in order to keep it in harmony with changes in political opinion. The dilemma of constitutional government is that a constitution that is too easy to change may lack the necessary weight to command respect from governments, and so become merely an instrument of party policy. On the other hand, a constitution that is too difficult to change becomes at best merely an adjunct of conservatism, and so is liable ultimately to be overthrown by violence by parties which have lost all feeling that it is *their* constitution. The method that a country adopts to resolve this dilemma will depend to a great extent on the way its constitution has evolved, and on the degree of respect that it has come to command in the country. The rigidity of the United States federal constitution has not up to now been an insuperable obstacle, precisely because it soon became and has remained an expression—the supreme expression—of that national unity, and because ways of circumventing obstacles to change were found, which did not destroy in people's minds its image as a symbol of stability as well as unity. The extreme flexibility of the British constitution has not up to now threatened its survival either, because no division between government and opposition parties has gone so deep as to tempt either to resort to violence in preference to constitutional methods of change.

In France, neither of these political attitudes exists or has existed over a long period of time. No constitution has ever been able to win the kind of wholehearted respect and loyalty that the American constitution evokes. And political parties have never trusted each other, as they have done in Britain, sufficiently to permit of the growth of a permanent habit of change by constitutional methods alone. The result has been that constitutional methods have always been on approval, to the extent that resort to violence has never been entirely excluded as inconceivable. At the back of Frenchmen's minds, there has always been the residual fear that, sooner or later, a political crisis can end by becoming a constitutional crisis. Familiarity with constitutional change by revolution has bred a kind of half-acceptance of it, and in some left-wing parties even a kind of romantic admiration for the idea of revolution.[8]

What these different constitutional backgrounds and attitudes reveal is the extent to which what a constitution can or cannot do is a product of a nation's political past. The only ultimate safeguard of constitutionality would seem to be the practice of it over a long period of time, and circumstances do not always permit this. Invasion, defeat in war, deep-seated and irreconcilable political divisions within a country—these can make the normal development of constitutional government very difficult, and even impossible. The United States and Great Britain have both been fortunate in that they have enjoyed long periods of

H

comparative invulnerability from external aggression and have been relatively free from the internal instability that deeply divided and extremist political parties can create. How much they owe the stability of their democratic and constitutional systems to good fortune, and how much to political good sense is a matter that can probably be judged only in the light of their response to future political problems that may impose greater strains on their governmental systems than they have hitherto encountered. What has been achieved is at least an accepted political way of life that the constitution itself now helps to protect, and the longer a constitution has lasted the more it ought, in theory, to be able to withstand political strains. In politics, nothing succeeds like success.

Since, however, constitutions are made by men and for men, there can never be any sure rule of thumb applicable to all conceivable circumstances. No constitution is proof against a successful *coup d'état* or a revolution. The most that governments can do is to try to ensure that the political situation never deteriorates to the point at which such developments become conceivable, and so ultimately possible. And this can be done only by building up and maintaining in normal everyday political life habits of respect for democratic and constitutional methods on the part of both governments and citizens. Good constitutions cannot make good democracies, but good democracies can make good use of constitutions.

7

Elections

It has been suggested in an earlier chapter that representative
institutions, including both parties and electoral systems, are
necessarily clumsy devices for ascertaining and recording political
opinions and for transmuting them into governmental and opposition programmes. They are also institutions whose effectiveness depends on political circumstances as much as on electoral
machinery. The idea that there is a perfect electoral system, or
one that is superior to all others, or suitable for universal use,
is purely academic. Behind any proposals put forward in favour
of a particular system there lie political assumptions, though
they are not always explicitly recognised. The kind of electoral
system chosen is, moreover, only a small part of the electoral
machinery. It is no less important to be clear about what an
electorate has the right to expect, or does in actual fact expect,
from its representatives, and also about the ways in which the
rules governing the conduct of elections can ensure that all

citizens have not merely an equal right to express their preferences, but also equal opportunities to do so.

What Is Represented?

Professor A. Phillips Griffiths has distinguished four main types of representation, and all four can have some relevance to the citizen's attitude to his representative, or to the representative's own conception of what his functions are. There is, first, what he calls 'descriptive representation', by which he means the choice as representative of someone who is regarded as 'a sample, specimen or analogue'.[1] This meaning is frequently used or implied in discussions about the current fashionable student theories of 'participation'. It usually implies that only students can represent students. It is a slipshod use of the term and is responsible for a great deal of misunderstanding. Carried to its logical conclusion, representation in this sense would require 'workers' (whatever that word may mean in electoral terms) to be represented only by other 'workers', teachers by teachers, bankers by bankers, and so on. Without carrying the argument to such a point of absurdity this conception of representation is, nevertheless, quite often supported in claims that committees, governments or legislatures should include more 'representatives' in the sense of 'samples' of particular categories of public opinion—the working class, or women (in the latter case, the demand is usually for *a* woman, to represent what is called '*the* woman's point of view'). This conception also underlies claims for functional representation (discussed later) alongside, or sometimes instead of, territorial representation, so that the elector can be represented not only as an individual but also as an industrial worker, an employer, a farmer and so on.

Professor Griffiths' second meaning of representation, called 'symbolic representation', is exemplified by the claim of a popularly elected President to 'represent', in the sense of symbolising or speaking for the nation. In the past, representation in this sense was politically important, since it was used by hereditary monarchs to justify their claim to think and act for the nation as well as to speak for it. In modern democratic States, the political functions of Heads of States are now carried out in accordance with constitutional rules and conventions. But there are still traces of the 'symbolic' element. The political weight of a President of the United States does not stem merely from the fact that he is the head of a government and a party as well as of the State, but also from the fact that he holds this office as the choice of the whole nation and, therefore, has the authority to speak for it in a sense not conferred by election to Congress. General de Gaulle specifically described himself as representing the State in this sense and refused to be associated with any party on the ground that his position was that of guardian of the Constitution and of arbitrator in the national interest, if necessary between parties. He also insisted that in order to be able to represent the State in this way, his successors ought to be elected by the whole nation—as he himself was re-elected in 1965.

What Professor Griffiths calls 'ascriptive representation'—that of an accredited spokesman, delegate, or agent, who negotiates and acts on behalf of others, irrespective of whether he is or is not sympathetic to their views—is not strictly relevant to political representation in developed countries. But the relationship between representative and represented in some colonial régimes is 'ascriptive'. When official nominees are appointed to sit in the legislature in order to represent certain elements of the population, as happens, for instance, in Rhodesia, such representatives do 'act' on behalf of the categories whose interests they are responsible for whenever they cast a vote.

The 'representation of interests'—Professor Griffiths' fourth category—is felt in all democratic systems to be part of the duty of an elected representative. But only part of it. British Members of Parliament, for example, usually state publicly, following the announcement of their election, that they regard themselves as representatives for the whole constituency, except in matters that specifically concern party policy. They defend the interests of constituents of any party who feel themselves to have some grievance, by asking questions in the House of Commons, or by direct requests to Ministers to investigate cases, and sometimes by trying to have grievances publicly ventilated in a debate in the House. In democratic countries generally, representatives defend dominant economic interests in the constituency, such as those of farmers, shipbuilders, car manufacturers, the unemployed, or they may consider themselves as self-appointed spokesmen for interests that have nothing to do with either party politics or the specific interests of the constituency, such as advertising, capital punishment, divorce-law reform or pacifism.

In the British system, these remain a secondary responsibility. The representative's first loyalty is to the party under whose label he has been elected. The constituency usually accepts this and, indeed, often demands the loyalty of the Member to party policies. But because democratic representatives still claim the basic right to think for themselves, they are still free to express their divergencies from the party, both inside and outside the House. They may even abstain from voting on issues on which they feel strongly. The Labour Party Constitution specifically recognises the right of party members to abstain on matters of conscience, though this right is not always interpreted by everybody in the same way. Representatives are, however, regarded as having normally both the moral and political responsibility to vote with their party even on issues on which they disagree with its policy, and at least not to vote against it on issues which the party regards as important.

This is not the situation of a representative either in France or in the United States. In a recently published American symposium on representation, J. L. Pennock distinguishes the following four conceptions of the duty of the representative towards his constituents:

1. The representative should act in support of what he believes an effective majority of his constituency desires.
2. The representative should act in support of what he believes is in the constituency's interest.
3. The representative should act in support of what he believes the nation (or an effective majority of it) desires.
4. The representative should act in support of what he believes is in the nation's interest.[2]

For the British representative, all four of these duties are merely different aspects of his responsibility to his party, since he is entitled to assume that the party policy on which he has been elected is regarded by those who voted for him as being what they want and what they believe to be in their interests. They, for their part, are entitled to assume that their representative believes that his party's policy is in the national interest.

In systems such as those in the United States, and to a lesser degree France, not only are parties more loosely organised, but the relations between executive and legislature are more complicated, and so there can be very real conflict between the conceptions of representation quoted above. In the United States, the two major parties are almost non-existent on the federal level between presidential elections. The representative's first loyalty is, therefore, to his constituency and his State, and a considerable amount of cross-voting in Congress is taken for granted. The pressure that Senators and Representatives can exert on the Administration can be very much greater than any that a minority in the British House of Commons could bring to bear on a government. It is, moreover, taken for granted by public opinion in both France and the United States that one of the major functions of the representative is to obtain favours or aid for the constituency. The satisfaction or refusal of such demands can be one of the American President's most powerful weapons in mobilising a majority in a recalcitrant Congress. For President and Congress may often represent opposing parties and, since each has a fixed term of office, they have somehow to learn to live together. In France, any Deputy who is also the mayor of a town or village in the constituency or a councillor in the *département* (and a high proportion of them are one or the other) is expected by his fellow citizens to look after local interests, and reminders to the electorate of services rendered to villages or towns or to the constituency as a whole are often persuasive arguments in the Deputy's campaign for re-election.

Whether party discipline is strict or lax, however, in all Western democracies the representative exercises what is called a 'free mandate', whereas, in Communist-dominated countries, the rule is that of the 'imperative mandate', the representative being wholly the servant of the party hierarchy. A 'free mandate' means that representatives are neither delegates nor agents of their party. Nor are they delegates or agents of any other interest or pressure group, although, in differing degrees in different countries, they consider it a part of their duty to speak in the legislature on behalf of such interests. They are free in the sense that their responsibility is only to their electors.

In both Germany and France, this principle of the 'free mandate' is included in the constitution. Article 38(1) of the Basic Law of the Federal German Republic states that deputies to the German *Bundestag* 'are representatives of the whole people, are not bound by orders and instructions and are subject only to their conscience.'

Article 27 of the French Constitution states that 'any imperative mandate to a Member of Parliament is null and void.' It was this article that President de Gaulle invoked as justifying his refusal to call a special session of Parliament in 1960. In his view, Deputies asking for it were acting under the instructions of a pressure group of farming interests, and this constituted an 'imperative mandate'. A House of Commons Resolution stated in 1947 that it was

> inconsistent with the duty of a member to his constituents, and with the maintenance of the privilege of freedom of speech, for any member of this House to enter into any contractual agreement with an outside body, controlling and limiting the member's complete independence and freedom of action in Parliament or stipulating that he shall act in any way as the representative of such outside body in regard to any matters to be transacted in Parliament[3].

Both British parties agree that party conferences cannot (despite the Labour Party theory that the conference makes policy) dictate to Members of Parliament, who are constitutionally responsible only to their electors.

How do representatives in democratic systems reconcile this 'free mandate' with loyalty to their party? The answer is that they do so by means of a complicated series of dialogues carried on simultaneously at different levels, with the aim of resolving conflicts of interests. 'The established, constitutionalised forms are the elections, the press campaign, the action of pressure groups and political parties, demonstrations, strikes, petitions. Every form is equally legitimate from the standpoint of representation, and no single one is by itself sufficient to achieve the aims of representation.'[4] There is no guarantee that these processes will always succeed, any more than there is any guarantee that democracy will survive. In normal circumstances, they do succeed, because it is in the interests of all that the party system shall not break down. And while this continues to be true, constituency and national party organisations are, in practice, interdependent. Certainly, in Great Britain, for a constituency party to choose independence from the party is to court electoral disaster. This is part of the price that the British public and their politicians pay for the strength and cohesion of a two-party system. In France and America, the price paid is less high. Representatives play a more independent political role, and so, in France, do political groups within the framework of government and opposition. The result is party systems that are less effective and national policies that are less coherent.

The essential difference between democratic and Communist representatives is that the latter cannot challenge the control of the party (except by revolution) and so there is no possiblity of a real dialogue. In a democracy, they can, and if enough individuals or groups come to feel that it is no longer in their interest to pay the price of party cohesion, then sooner or later they will weaken it, and perhaps destroy it. Democratic party control is based on consent, not compulsion, and so, like democracy itself, is vulnerable. The complicated process of representation that has been summarised in this chapter provides a number of safety-valves lacking in Communist and other one-party systems. The strength of democracy is that the constant interchange of opinion and interaction of different pressures enables the system to bend so often and in so many ways that a stable democracy does not easily break.

What Is a 'Democratic' Electoral System?

If, in practice, the principal right of electors is to choose their representatives and to maintain contacts with them, it is essential that the conditions of choice should as far as possible ensure equality between voters, and equal freedom for would-be candidates to present themselves to the electors. In all but a very few countries, the rules governing the right to vote now makes no distinctions on grounds of wealth, property, education, religion, colour or sex, though all of these have been used in the past to restrict the right to vote, or to render ineffective in practice rights granted by law. In South Africa, Rhodesia and Portuguese overseas territories, racial distinctions still exist. And in Switzerland, as has already been said, women still do not vote at all in federal elections, and have only recently been given the right to vote in some local elections.

The general rule, then, in democratic countries and in all the newly independent African countries is direct and universal suffrage. It is essential, therefore, that the detailed rules providing for the conduct of elections should, as far as reasonably possible, not impose conditions that, in practice, introduce inequalities. This is not an easy task. Electoral machinery reveals more clearly than almost any other democratic institution the difficulties and contradictions that arise in the process of translating theory into practice. Even in this very circumscribed area, there is no unanimity in democracies, either on the criteria that such rules ought to satisfy, or on the best ways to eliminate inequalities.

In his *Grammar of Politics*, published over 30 years ago, Harold Laski laid down four essential conditions that a democratic electoral system ought to fulfil. The first was that the legislature should embody the opinion of the majority and the minority on great issues of public interest; the second, that constituent areas should be small enough for candidates to get to know their constituents; the third, that there must be regular machinery between elections for maintaining contacts with movements of opinion; and the fourth, that voters must be as directly related as possible to the government in power.[5] The last three can be criticised on the ground that they can be effectively fulfilled only in single-member constituencies. Indeed, they are applicable only in circumstances such as exist under the British two-party system. The first condition is relevant to all democratic elections, whether under a proportional or a majority system.

For an election to result in the emergence of clear majority and minority opinions, however, the electorate must be organised in such a way as to make a real choice possible, and it is necessary to be quite clear about what is actually being chosen. Electors are not choosing between 'great issues of public interest', or indeed between issues of any kind, because an election does not provide machinery to enable them to do this. They are choosing between specific candidates and parties contesting the election, and it is the parties that choose the issues. They offer the electors a package deal, in which a great many important issues are left undiscussed, and they do not always give very specific undertakings on those that are discussed. At best, electors are choosing which of two or more parties they would prefer to govern for the next few years.

Every party in the legislature, whether a majority or a minority, represents, therefore, a heterogeneous agglomeration of disparate views, because only a limited number of issues have been discussed, and there are no means of discovering with any degree of certainty what individual calculations of pros and cons have determined any individual vote. The winning side may include as many disappointed electors as the losing side. Phrases such as 'what the majority thinks' are merely a kind of speculative shorthand, indicating, on the basis of what was said or written during the campaign, what anybody is entitled to regard as the dominant preoccupations of the majority of voters. The only certainty is that a definite number of electors chose x instead of y or z, and that x is usually a member of a party whose leaders have made some pledges as to what they will do or try to do if they obtain power.

For a system to be entitled to call itself democratic, this choice must be between two or more candidates, in order to enable the elector to express preferences. It must also be made in conditions as nearly equal for all contestants as is reasonably possible. To ensure this, at least four conditions ought to be met. The first is that no sane and law-abiding citizen should be debarred from being a candidate, if there is any reasonable chance of his obtaining significant support. Both qualifications are important. Total freedom of candidature could result in such a profusion of candidates that the whole purpose of the election would be defeated, because no majority for any coherent policy would be apparent or obtainable. The United Kingdom, up to 1918, and the Third French Republic did not restrict candidatures, and the result was that freaks, jokers and eccentrics with no serious purpose presented themselves. Certain restrictions can be defended, therefore, as long as they are intended to provide conditions in which real choice is possible, and do not discriminate against serious candidates. For instance, to ban a political party would be demonstrably undemocratic, unless its policy were to make the democratic system itself unworkable. In Germany, the Communist Party is banned precisely on the ground that it is not a democratic party and the constitution (Art. 9.2) requires all parties to be democratic.

The criterion usually adopted is to require prospective candidates to furnish some evidence of public support in the form of a prescribed number of signatures supporting their nomination, and some evidence of their seriousness of purpose in the form of the deposit of a sum of money—the deposit being returnable unless they fail to poll a required percentage of the total vote. This safeguard can be criticised on strictly egalitarian grounds as discriminating in favour of rich eccentrics who are prepared to waste their money, and against poor politicians who cannot even raise the amount of the deposit. It has certainly not entirely eliminated freak candidates, either in Britain or in France. It has equally certainly discouraged many, and the financial hardship imposed by the deposit system is, in most cases, negligible, since supporters in the constituency or the party can advance the money in the confident expectation of getting it back, unless the candidate obtains very little support —in which case, it can be argued that that is precisely the type of candidature that the deposit system seeks to discourage. It is not a perfect system, but it is difficult to find an alternative method that is not open to more serious objections. The American system of primary elections, for example, though it eliminates the difficulty in theory by substituting the choice of candidate to the whole electorate, or to a party electorate, tends to make candidates in practice more subject to control by the party machine.[6]

The second condition is that the ballot must be secret, so that no pressures can be exerted to induce any elector to vote for, or abstain from voting for, a particular candidate. This is now the general rule in democracies, and it is noteworthy that Hitler abolished it in Germany precisely in order to exert such pressure. It is not always easy, however, to provide electoral machinery that ensures absolute secrecy in actual fact. In countries such as France much of the voting and counting take place in village or district polling stations serving electorates so small that officials and voters all know each other, and good guesses can be made as to who has or has not voted for whom.

The third condition is that there should be a rough equality (one cannot reasonably ask for more than that) of basic electoral facilities within constituencies. This requirement would cover such things as nearness of polling stations to voters' homes, information regarding times and places of voting, together with some indication of what the candidates stand for. The simplest ways of meeting these requirements are to give candidates the right to send the basic relevant information, post-free, to electors' homes and for the State to provide facilities for statements by candidates on public hoardings. Here again, however, satisfying one condition sometimes involves failing to satisfy another. If, for instance, constituency boundaries are to be drawn, as they usually are, with the aim of maintaining a rough equality between either populations or electors, then it follows that they will differ greatly in area. France tries to ensure that all constituencies include both urban and rural areas. Britain believes that constituency boundaries should also be the boundaries of local-government areas. To satisfy all these desiderata is not possible. Less populous areas of necessity involve longer journeys to the poll or fewer electors per member or both. For constituency and local-government boundaries to coincide, it may be necessary to accept inequalities in size, imbalance of rural and urban elements, and so on.

The fourth condition is that there should be equality of campaigning conditions. This is possibly the most difficult condition to fulfil satisfactorily. The most important criteria in modern times are limitations on candidates' expenditure on an election campaign, the existence of effective legal provisions making bribery and corruption both very difficult and punishable in the courts, and the provision of equal facilities for parties to appeal to the general public through the mass media of radio and television. Where these are State-controlled, this is possible, and in both Britain and France equality is ensured during election campaigns by understandings between the parties and the radio and television authorities (and in Great Britain by the acceptance of similar arrangements by independent television authorities). In the United States, however, where radio and television are privately owned, politicians can buy time on the air, and in France, politicians can speak to their compatriots from commercial stations outside French frontiers. Germany subsidises political parties, Great Britain does not, but candidates' expenses are strictly controlled, while in France and the United States they are not. In all countries, private resources, including party funds, can, of course, also do a great deal to promote the political interests of a party between elections, and it is impossible to envisage measures that would prevent this without imposing restrictions on freedom of opinion, of the press and of assembly that no democracy would tolerate.

Proportional or Majority Systems?

If the choice offered to electors is as limited as has been suggested in the preceding pages, does it really matter very much by what electoral system candidates are elected? The short answer to this question is that a great many people feel very strongly that it does, and this fact in itself must, therefore, in a democracy, give the subject some importance. If account is taken of all the variants that can be introduced, the number of electoral systems is bewilderingly large. They can be reduced, however, to two main types, the proportional and the majority systems. A majority system is not synonymous with a two-party system, though it usually works more satisfactorily if there are only two main parties. It is a system in which one person or one list of candidates is elected at a time in each constituency, by a relative majority if there is no absolute majority. It can have a number of variants. In a two-ballot system, an absolute majority of the votes is required for election at the first ballot, and a relative majority only at the second. In a list system, electors in multi-member constituencies choose between party lists, each elector having, in most countries, as many votes as there are seats to be filled. The alternative vote allows electors to express a second preference. If no candidate obtains an absolute majority, then the candidate with the lowest total is eliminated and the second preferences of electors who voted for him are distributed among the remaining candidates. This process goes on until one candidate gets an absolute majority. The effect is similar to that produced by the second ballot, but the alternative–vote device saves time, and requires that any bargaining between parties take place before the poll instead of between ballots. It has two obvious disadvantages. First, the elector's second preference has to be made in ignorance of the situation in which it may be used. When he knows the results of the ballot, he might well wish he had expressed a different preference. And second, there is no logical reason for counting only the bottom candidate's second preferences as being equal to first preferences.

Proportional representation means the election of candidates in large, multi-member constituencies, by some system that ensures a strict mathematical proportionality between the number of seats won by candidates or parties in a given constituency and the number of votes cast for them.

Two or more parties can contest the election, whichever type of system is used. But in a proportional system minorities stand a far better chance of winning seats. In a majority system, it is possible for a party to obtain a large number of votes over the country as a whole (as the British Liberal Party regularly does) and to have either no seats at all or only a handful. In the United States, Great Britain, New Zealand, the Australian House of Representatives, South Africa and Canada, the majority system is used, and all but Australia and Canada have only two main parties. Continental West-European countries use proportional systems and have more than two parties. France has used both types and has never had as few as two parties. Nor have frequent changes of electoral system made any significant difference to the number of parties. France has, indeed, had a much longer history of electoral controversy and experiment than any other country. French governments have produced a number of ingenious (and often highly complicated) systems combining some kind of proportional principle with devices providing a sufficient degree of disproportionality to ensure some kind of majority. But these efforts to discover a system that would produce 'assemblies that accurately reflected the divisions of the electorate and parties that were stable, disciplined and responsible'[7] have not met with much success.

Both types of system have their passionate defenders and their no less passionate opponents. On both sides there are partisans so committed that they are unable to admit the merits of the other side. One of the foremost British experts on electoral systems, J. F. S. Ross, has complained that 'the discussion of electoral systems is apt to be much hindered, and its effectiveness seriously impaired, by the importation into it of three disturbing influences: party prejudice, confusion between ends and means, and sheer ignorance.'[8] This statement is in itself an example of confusion of ends and means, and of confusion or misconception regarding what electoral systems can and cannot do. Mr Ross is known as one of the most eloquent defenders of a system of proportional representation that has always been rejected by the majority of his compatriots. He feels that if once people 'really grasped the nature of the issue, most democratically-minded people would become convinced upholders' of the system that he is defending. Which merely means that, like many other defenders of a cause that they fervently believe in, he regards those who disagree with him as ignorant or biased. In reality, no electoral system can usefully be discussed with the kind of objectivity that divorces electoral and political considerations. And political considerations must include what Mr Ross calls 'party prejudice', because that is part of the *raison d'être* of parties.

The fairly general belief in Anglo-Saxon countries that the majority system is in some way natural and right has been defended by Professor Duverger in his well-known book on political parties. He argues that

> the two-party system seems natural in the sense that political options are usually presented in a dualist form. There are not always two parties; but there are almost always two tendencies. ... Whenever public opinion is faced with important basic problems, it tends to crystallise round two opposing poles. The natural movement of society is towards two parties.[9]

If this is so, then it is necessary to explain why the majority system is found mainly in English-speaking countries that have been at one time or another British possessions. Professor Duverger rejects a number of facile explanations, such as the influence of Anglo-Saxon 'national character', or 'the sporting spirit of the British people which leads it to regard political contests as matches between rival teams'.[10] He also rejects the suggestion put forward by Winston Churchill that the rectangular shape of the House of Commons has had something to do with it.

His own explanation is that the electoral system itself tends to determine whether countries have two-party or multi-party systems. It is an attractive thesis but not very convincing. He has to explain away a number of 'exceptions', which he does very plausibly, but it could equally plausibly be argued that it is the party system that is the determining factor in the choice of an electoral system, rather than the reverse, that where countries have achieved stable government under a particular electoral system, it, too, tends to be stable, and that where stable government has proved unachievable, the electoral as well as the party system may reflect this instability. Whatever the reasons for the adoption of one system rather than another, however, and these are not always discoverable, supporters of each can claim advantages for it and point out the disadvantages of the other.

The majority system, whether with one or two ballots, or

with single-member or multi-member constituencies, is credited with three main advantages. First, it is clear and simple. The elector does not have to cope with any complicated mathematical calculations. There are no quotients or remainders or preferential votes. He simply votes for the candidate (or in multi-member constituencies for the party list) of his choice, and the candidate (or list) with most votes is elected. In the country as a whole, the party with the most seats forms the government, or, if it has not an absolute majority, forms a coalition with acceptable partners. In two-party systems, the leader of the majority party heads the government and the leader of the losing party is the shadow leader, his party constituting an alternative government.

The second advantage claimed for the majority system is that it is no less clear and simple for those who are elected. The government party knows that it alone will be held responsible by the elector for what it does.[11] In a two-party system, governments can begin by blaming their predecessors for the situation that they have inherited. But this ceases to be a credible excuse after a period of some months, and they then have to stand or fall on the basis of their own performance. The single-member constituency can provide a channel for a dialogue between representatives and electors that is in reality a debate between government and opposition points of view. There is no such direct relationship between parties and electors under a proportional system. The third advantage is that a two-party system encourages political thinking in terms of power. Parties must try to reach compromises within their own ranks in order to avoid presenting a disunited front to the electorate.

The main disadvantage of the majority system, and the one that is always emphasised by supporters of proportional systems, is that it is liable to result in a gross disproportion between votes and seats, a disproportion that can be further exaggerated if one or two minority parties contest a significant number of seats. Nor can this disproportion necessarily be eliminated, or even greatly reduced, by devices such as the alternative vote or the second ballot. David Butler has claimed that if the alternative vote had been used in every British election from 1918 onward, in almost all except that of 1950 the strength of the majority would have been even more exaggerated than it actually was.[12] This calculation cannot, of course, be verified, since it is not possible to know exactly how many second preferences would have gone to each major party. Supporters of proportional systems claim to mirror opinion accurately. This, it is argued, means that minorities get a hearing, in proportion to their numerical strength in the country.

Opponents argue that encouraging minority representation encourages minority thinking, and so leads to a multiplicity of parties, some of which will have far too small a representation to do anything but sell their votes to the highest bidder. To which supporters can reply that a multiplicity of parties exists also in countries that use majority systems, and that all that proportional representation does is to reflect existing tendencies, more accurately. The example of Tasmania is often quoted, which, with over half a century of proportional representation, has an unchanged number of parties.[13] The number of parties has also remained the same in France, although between 1875 and 1969 there were eight changes of electoral system, and 25 elections, of which 17 were fought on the majority system with two ballots, one on a one-ballot list system, and seven on different proportional or quasi-proportional systems.

Another disadvantage of an established two-party system, according to supporters of proportional systems, is that the tremendous resources needed to compete with two monolithic parties make the emergence of any third party almost impossible. It took 45 years for the Labour Party to become a majority party. Supporters of the two-party system would consider this an advantage, since, it compels parties to reach compromises within their own ranks, and so prevents the proliferation of parties that proportional systems are believed by many to encourage. Supporters of the proportional system known as the 'single transferable vote' argue in its favour that it helps to reduce the domination of party machines,[14] while opponents can argue that the party-list system which is more frequently used, entails, on the contrary, increased domination by party machines, owing to the need to organise support for rival parties in large multi-member constituencies. The larger constituencies also reduce the possibilities of personal contacts between electors and representatives that Harold Laski believed—and many with him —to be essential to an effective democratic system.[15]

The truth is that in this unending debate on the merits and demerits of the two types of electoral system, neither side can either prove its own case or disprove its opponent's, for two very simple reasons. The first is that any electoral system is, even more than any party organisation, essentially a clumsy device for ascertaining and recording opinions. Whether they are reflected with more or less accuracy, only those opinions can be directly represented that are specifically presented to the electors by candidates and parties. If these turn out to be divorced from the main preoccupation of governments, then the tendencies so faithfully reflected may receive no more attention than they would have done under a two-party system. But the representatives will also have votes on all other issues that come before the legislature. For example, in 1956, some 50 Poujadists were returned to the French National Assembly as representatives of the interests of small tradesmen. There is no evidence of their having achieved anything significant in that field, but they certainly voted to keep Algeria French, which was not what they were elected to do. If a country with a proportional system of election has a legislature including minority groups representing farmers, Catholics, supporters of provincial autonomy and defenders of the interests of tax-payers and small tradesmen, while the government is occupied with problems of devaluation and deflation, the reform of social security and the reduction of defence estimates, then what precise representative value to those who elected them have the votes of these minority groups on these issues?

What no electoral system can do is to reflect accurately the conflicting and shifting tendencies *within* each party or group that presents itself to the electors, much less those opinions that are not, as such, politically organised at all. Consumers are certainly under-represented in our modern society, and are likely to remain so, unless some method of organising them politically can be discovered. Moreover, the electoral system is not always the best way to represent minority interests. Nor is there any guarantee that quantitative, or mathematical representation of opinion is necessarily more effective than qualitiative representation. It is arguable, for instance, that the 'anti-hanging' lobby would have had far less influence on the Labour Party than it actually did (thanks to the able advocacy of one or two Labour Party members), if it had been organised, as Scottish or Welsh Nationalists are, as a separate political tendency.

An electoral system, then, is not capable of providing a microcosm of national opinion. 'Elections', said Giovanni Sartori, 'are a discontinuous and very elementary performance.'[16] It is a mistake, therefore, to expect too much of them.

The second and more important reason why there is no answer to the question: Which is the better or the more democratic system of election? is that the choice is more often than not neither logical nor deliberate, but imposed by habit or by political necessities. A proportional system may be politically unavoidable in countries in which racial, linguistic or religious groups fear either repression or the loss of their identity, unless they are assured of separate representation. It may be politically desirable, and at the same time politically impossible, to introduce proportional representation in a country in which one majority party is consistently dominant, leaving all others in an apparently permanent minority. What finally makes one country prefer, and praise as more democratic, a system that enables a choice to be made between rival possibilities rather than rival desirabilities, is a question that political scientists cannot yet answer satisfactorily.

Ancillary Devices

The inadequacy of electoral systems no doubt helps to explain why a number of democratic systems provide for some degree of direct government, or seek to supplement their representative system in some other way. The attraction of the referendum is partly explained by the persistence of the illusion that direct government is in some way a purer form of democracy than representative government. France and, in practice, the United States, both elect the President by universal suffrage, and a number of countries—in particular, Switzerland, Italy, Australia and France—provide for the use of the referendum or the initiative, or both.

The referendum and the initiative can supplement representative institutions by providing for expressions of opinion on single issues between elections, and can make the whole electorate the final judge on measures for which a government might be regarded as having no clear mandate, or on those, such as constitutional amendment, which are so important that it might be thought proper to give every citizen the right to express his opinion. Thus, some countries make the submission of constitutional amendment to a referendum either obligatory or optional. Italy, France and Australia also provide for the optional submission of ordinary laws to a referendum, and both Italy and Switzerland provide for the initiative in legislation. In neither the United States (at the federal level) nor Great Britain is there any provision for the referendum or for the initiative.

Despite the attractiveness of the referendum in theory, its practical disadvantages are considerable. Where the measure to be submitted is technical or highly complex, it may not be possible to phrase the question put to the electorate in terms that permit of a meaningful reply of Yes or No. For many people, the only reply might be 'Yes-but', or 'Yes-if', and a measure including strings of alternative conditions is not a practicable proposition. Nor would a mass electorate be capable of expressing an opinion on a complex proposal without being organised to do so by information and propaganda supplied by either political parties or interest groups. There are, therefore, far greater possibilities for the manipulation of opinion by interested parties or by demagogues, because an electorate of millions is more easily misled than a representative assembly. This is a fact that dictators and would-be dictators have discovered, and that has led them to use the referendum to disguise as democratic consent a verdict intended to legitimise personal rule. In opposing a proposal by Winston Churchill for a referendum in 1945, Clement Attlee pointed out that the referendum had 'only too often been the instrument of Nazism and Fascism'[17], and explicitly mentioned Hitler's use of it.

Even without any dictatorial intentions on the part of those holding a referendum, it can be used to secure, by means of a package deal asking for a single Yes or No, powers that only a public less politically aware than a legislative assembly would normally be prepared to grant. The opportunities for deliberate manipulation are, of course, far greater in a dictatorship, as was illustrated by an account of a referendum in Spain, published in 1966, in which the authorities were said to have distributed completed voting papers with a red SI (yes) clearly visible through the folded paper, to have failed to provide any real privacy in polling booths, and to have threatened civil servants with dismissal and workers with loss of pay if they abstained from voting. In the circumstances, it was hardly surprising that the official figures showed a turn-out of 88.5 per cent of whom 95 per cent voted YES.[18]

Another objection to the referendum is that the by-passing of the representative organs deprives the public of the normal methods by which opinion can be ventilated and political leadership provided, and so tends to produce results emphasising more timid and conservative views. This was certainly the experience of the Weimar Republic, and perhaps because of this experience, Federal Germany did not include provisions for the use of the referendum in the 1949 Basic Law. It has often been claimed that, if the British public had been consulted by referendum on the introduction of the experimental period during which hanging was suspended or on the grant of full suffrage to women, both proposals would have been defeated, not so much through conviction as through ignorance. Yet once Parliament had taken the responsibility for the experiment, public opinion evolved in the light of the experience.

A criticism of both the referendum and the initiative is that either, if used on any considerable scale, could be recipes for making normal democratic government unworkable. Most legislative proposals cannot usefully be considered in isolation from each other, or outside the context of a general governmental programme, whose different items are necessarily financially and administratively interdependent. If budgets are to be balanced, more of one item normally means less of another. Since decisions taken by the electorate are made by heterogeneous majorities, it is perfectly possible for them to be incompatible with each other. A decision, for example, to make massive reductions in defence forces, could be followed by another providing for greatly increased uses of military forces in various theatres abroad, or a decision providing for a reduction in taxation could be followed by an ambitious plan for great increases in social security and State pensions. The initiative, if it means that requests from a certain number of citizens for a specific Bill make it obligatory on the legislature to consider it, could slow down the whole process of government by imposing on a legislature futile and time-wasting debate on unrealistic measures.

What these arguments amount to is the claim that the number of questions capable of being decided outside a legislature is very small. Legislation is at the same time too specialised and too general to be suitable for submission to a decision by the general public. It is too specialised because 'You can amend and alter in a legislative assembly: you cannot amend and alter when your legislative assembly consists of millions of members.'[19] It is too general because particular measures cannot be divorced from a general governmental programme without impairing the efficiency of a government as well as blurring its responsibility, which is one of the basic principles of democratic government. These factors no doubt help to explain why countries that provide for the use of the referendum or the initiative usually make resort to them optional, and make relatively little use of them in practice (with the notable exception of Switzerland) except on constitutional issues, which are not expected to come up very frequently.

Another device which has also been suggested at different times is that of functional representation. Again, the theory is attractive. It could logically be assumed that many people who are not interested in national politics are vitally interested in, and also more knowledgeable about, those parts of it that directly affect their working lives. When it comes to putting the theory into practice, however, the difficulties are considerable. To begin with, there is the problem of deciding which functions or interests are to be represented, and in what proportions. Then there is the difficulty of finding a suitable method of choosing representatives. An assembly chosen largely by employers' associations, trade unions and professional associations (which is the usual method in the few democracies that have taken up the idea) is no more than an agglomeration of rival vested interests. If its members are nominated by the government, then it no longer has the authority of a representative assembly. It is significant that those countries that have functional assemblies have made them advisory, which indicates that there is no strong desire for them to play any major role. Nor has their advice made much impact. This was to be expected, since members of a functional assembly are made up of different interest groups, each of which can claim some expertise in its own field (in which it also, of course, has a vested interest), but has no special competence in any other. Decisions of such an assembly tend, therefore, either to be made along normal party lines, in which case they have less authority than those of the legislative assembly, or else to be purely technical, in which case they are by nature only advisory, for only the directly elected legislature has the authority to judge the general and political implications of any legislative proposal.

One other device for supplementing the normal representative machinery ought, perhaps, to be briefly mentioned, although it is, in practice, very little used in democratic government, and not at all on the national level. This is the recall of representatives by their constituents, if their activities are criticised. The obvious objection to the method is that it can transform the representative into a delegate, a mere 'rubber stamp', at the mercy of the best organised and most vociferous sections of the community. In the few States of the U.S. that have applied the system to elected officials the result is said to have been the creation of 'a timorous and servile spirit.'[20] It is both undesirable and unnecessary on the national level, since the party under whose label a representative has been elected is perfectly capable of dealing with cases of misbehaviour, neglect of duty, betrayal of pledges or disloyalty to the party by withdrawing its endorsement of the offender, or expelling him from the party. On the other hand, if a constituency party is determined for any reason to get rid of its representative, however politically undesirable this may be, it must, in a democracy, be free to ask him to resign. In Great Britain, he is not constitutionally required to do so, but he may feel morally compelled to respect the wishes of his constituents, instead of waiting for them to refuse to re-adopt him as their candidate.

If, as the preceding pages suggest, the working of electoral systems is open to criticisms on a number of counts, it is equally clear that neither the ancillary devices that have been proposed and sometimes tried, nor any radical change in the electoral system itself is likely to remedy these weaknesses. If the verdicts of electorates can be distorted, unclear, volatile and contradictory, the remedy is not to overhaul the whole clumsy machine, but to look elsewhere for a solution to the problems. The essence of legislation is in the mass of detail through which it is applied, and this few members of the electorate have the time, desire or ability to study. But it is at this point, as well as in general debate in the legislature, that governments and representatives can best be made responsive to a public opinion that is articulate and vigorous enough to assert itself. The key question as H. D. Lasswell has put it, 'turns on accountability.'[21]

8

Systems of Government

A majority, held in restraint by constitutional checks and limitations, and always changing easily, with deliberate changes of popular opinions and sentiments, is the only true sovereign of a free people.

Abraham Lincoln, First Inaugural Address, 4 March 1861

The independence of the legislative and executive powers is the specific quality of Presidential government, just as their fusion and combination is the precise principle of Cabinet government.

Walter Bagehot, The English Constitution

Obviously, the majority itself cannot continuously rule, in any society larger than a town meeting, but democracy surely requires that the majority should really control those who do rule.

C. B. Macpherson, The Real World of Democracy

Law is the name we give to the rights we admit for others. Freedom is the name we give to the rights we demand for ourselves.

Quintin Hogg, at Trinity College, Dublin, 6 December 1969.

The Variety of Democratic Systems

All supporters of representative democracy can agree on the principle that the essence of democratic government is the accountability of governments and legislatures to the electorate. Unfortunately, there is no agreement on the best way of obtaining this, hence the variety of democratic systems. Accountability means the periodic renewal of representatives, but how often? A majority and a government need time to allow them to prove their worth or, alternatively, enough rope to hang themselves with at the next election, but not so long a period that they can become seriously out of touch with the electorate. Legislatures are usually chosen for periods of between two and five years, the first period being regarded by most countries as too short, the second as being sometimes too long. So the further question arises as to whether the period should be fixed, or capable of being curtailed by dissolution. In the United States, both executive and legislature are chosen for fixed periods. In the Third and Fourth French Republics, dissolution was provided for in the constitution, but in certain specified conditions that, in practice, prevented it from being resorted to more than once during the lifetime of each régime, that is twice in 76 years. Holland, too, has had only two dissolutions this century (in 1933 and 1958) and Sweden only one (in 1921). In Federal Germany, dissolution is possible only if the *Bundestag* is unable to provide an alternative to a defeated government. In the Fifth French Republic, the President can dissolve the National Assembly, but is then prohibited by the Constitution from dissolving it again for twelve months, and he cannot dissolve it at all during a state of emergency, as defined by the Constitution. In Great Britain, the Prime Minister can, in theory, request a dissolution (which by constitutional convention the Monarch is obliged to grant) at any time. In practice, he normally respects certain conventions and is limited, too, to some extent by political circumstances. In the older Commonwealth countries too, and also in Ireland, governments are free to dissolve the legislature.

There is no more agreement among democracies on the best form of government. Some are monarchies, others republics. Nearly all have two legislative chambers, but a few have only one, and, in bi-cameral systems, the kinds of chamber vary widely. There are great variations, too, in the relations between legislature and executive. In the majority of democratic systems, ministers are selected from the legislature, but in some, membership of the legislature is incompatible with membership of the government.

It is impossible to prove that one form of democratic government is more democratic than another. It is sometimes impossible to discover why one form of government has been chosen rather than another. History, tradition, and convenience have often had more to do with the choice than have logic or political theories. Nothing demonstrates these points more clearly than the varying provisions in democratic systems for second chambers. There is no agreement on why a second chamber should be necessary, except in Federal States, where the need is self-evident; second chambers are there to safeguard the identity and interests of the constituent States. They are, therefore, chosen to represent the States, and yet no two are alike. In the United States, Switzerland and Australia, representation is on a basis of State equality, while in Federal Germany, it is weighted in accordance with the population. In the United States, the Senate is a coordinate legislative body which is unique in having acquired more prestige than the lower House,[1] while in Australia, in spite of the fact that both Houses are directly elected and that the consent of both is required for legislation, the Senate is, in practice, subordinate to the House of Representatives, in that governments regard themselves as being accountable only to the latter. Switzerland can hardly be regarded as a bi-cameral system in the normal understanding of the term, since the Council of States and the National Council (which is elected on a population basis) often sit and vote together, and the functions of the two Houses are not clearly differentiated.

In unitary States, there is no such self-evident need for a second chamber. Though most developed States have one, there is no agreement on what ought to be either their composition or their functions. They can be nominated or partially nominated, directly or indirectly elected. They may represent local-government areas or vocational interests, play an important political role or be little more than advisory bodies, of whose advice little notice may be taken. In all this diversity, it is possible to discern four functions that are generally regarded as justifying the existence of second chambers. They are, first, their role in the legislative process; second, the supervision in some degree of the lower House, by means either of a legislative veto or of a delaying power; third, the representation of opinion in a somewhat different way from its representation in the lower House; and finally, the ventilation of issues of special interest that the lower House has either no time for, or no inclination to deal with, or that cut across party lines.

Each of these functions can mean something different in different countries, and there is rarely any logical relationship between the actual functions performed by any second chamber and the status or prestige that it enjoys. For instance, if both Houses have equal legislative powers, it would seem logical for governments in parliamentary systems to regard themselves as responsible to both Houses. And if both Houses are elected on a democratic basis, then it would seem equally logical for them both to claim the right to control the executive. In practice, in all democratic systems except those of the United States and Switzerland, the upper House is regarded as being subordinate and accepts that status. Claims that a second chamber ought to be able to exercise at least a partial legislative veto are sometimes supported on the ground of its representative character—perhaps because it represents local and regional opinion, or because its tenure is longer than that of the lower House, or, if it has a system of partial renewal, because it provides greater continuity or more independence of mind and can, therefore, constitute a stabilising factor, and so reduce the risk of rash and possibly ephemeral movements of opinion in the lower House. But exactly the same arguments have been used to prove the opposite case. One of the main arguments against the power of the French Senate under the Third Republic to veto legislation was that up to a third of the Senators might have been elected nearly nine years earlier by mayors and local councillors, some of whom had themselves been elected nearly five years earlier. Senators could thus be representing opinions of up to fourteen years earlier.

The truth is that it is not logic or political theory but the changing political climate, together with the practical difficulty that any government would encounter if it were to regard itself as accountable to two Houses whose majorities might differ, that have been responsible for the general acceptance of the subordination of the upper House to the lower, and for the reduction in some countries of the functions of the upper House to those of amending and revising legislation without being able to veto it. In both France and Britain, the upper House can now be overridden by the lower after a brief period, if attempts to secure agreement or compromise on a Bill have failed. In other words, the upper House no longer has any effective power, except when circumstances give special importance to the power to delay. All it can really do is to provide a short breathing space that permits of second thought.

Second thoughts can, of course, sometimes be useful, particularly if the upper House does in reality reflect serious currents of public opinion of which the lower House has been unaware, or has preferred to ignore. It is not surprising, however, in such circumstances, that many people should find it illogical to attach importance to the representative character of an upper House, and, indeed, Great Britain does not do so. Membership of the House of Lords is hereditary, though, since 1958, it has included a numerically small, but politically active, nominated element. There is no significant pressure from any quarter for the House to be made elective, precisely because this would risk increasing its authority. In France, on the other hand, public opinion is at one and the same time in favour of the present reduced powers of the Senate, compared with those under the Third Republic, and also of the retention of its present elective character, including the heavy over-weighting of the representation of small villages. This is an anachronism in modern France. And yet an attempt by the government in 1969 to transform the Senate into a partially nominated body, with economic advisory functions, in addition to general legislative functions, was defeated in a referendum, in which the majority chose to keep the Senate as it was, even at the cost of losing General de Gaulle.

Both in France and in Great Britain, attitudes to the second chamber are the result of national political habits rather than reasoned argument. The House of Lords is by general admission an anachronism in a modern democracy. Yet its contribution to legislation is regarded, even by some of those on the Left who, for political reasons, object to the survival of an unrepresentative and class-based chamber, as being very useful. And the quality of its nominated personnel has added both to its prestige and to its capacity to discharge the fourth function of second chambers, the provision of informed public debate on important political issues. Its evolution has been neither logical nor intentional, but has taken place owing to *ad hoc* responses to particular problems. This process can go on as long as the survival of the House of Lords continues to be generally convenient, and as long as the parties are unable to agree on a more suitable alternative. The House of Peers may still—to adapt Gilbert's verse—do nothing in particular and do it very well, but the explanation of that fact is not that it is there on account of its expertise and usefulness. It has acquired both by being there.

Parliamentary and Presidential Systems

Whatever the formal differences between democratic systems, the key question for democrats in all of them must be the nature of the relationship between the three main organs of government—legislature, executive and judiciary—for it is this that determines where the line is drawn in the attempt to ensure that governments have neither too much nor too little freedom of action. Abraham Lincoln feared that inability to draw the line in the right place might prove to be an inherent weakness of democracies. 'Must a Government', he asked, 'of necessity be too strong for the liberties of its own people, or too weak to maintain its own existence?'[5]

Democracies have approached the problem in one or other of two main ways. The parliamentary system is characteristic of British democracy and of the former British Dominions, as well as of European democracies. What has been called the 'presidential' system is that of the United States, though some features of it have been adopted by other countries. The two main principles of the American system are, first, the restriction of the exercise of power by its distribution between the three organs of government in such a way that no one organ becomes dominant, but no one is wholly dependent on an other, and, second, the direct election by the whole nation of the President, who is both Head of State and head of the government. It is possible to have a President who is elected by the nation in a parliamentary system, as the Fifth French Republic does. It is possible to have a system in which there is a partial separation of powers, without a President, which is the position in Switzerland.[6]

The vital distinction between this system and that of parliamentary government is the separation of powers. The Founding Fathers wanted to limit the scope of the federal government because they were, above all, anxious to prevent it from encroaching on the rights of the States. They were also afraid that a popularly elected assembly would abuse its powers unless positive steps were taken to prevent this from happening. The solution to their problems was the 'separation', or 'sharing out' of powers between the different organs of government, as suggested by Montesquieu in 1748, in order to prevent tyranny, which, for him, really meant the absolute power possessed at that time by the French monarchy. In his classic statement on this subject, Montesquieu claimed that

> When legislative power is united with executive power in the same person or body of magistrates, there is no liberty, because it is to be feared that the same monarch or the same senate will make tyrannical laws in order to execute them tyrannically. There is no liberty either, where judicial power is not separated from both legislative and executive power. If judicial and legislative power are not separated, power over the life and liberty of citizens would be arbitrary, because the judge would also be legislator. If it were not separated from executive power, the judge would have the strength of an oppressor. All would be lost if the same men, or the same body of chief citizens, or the nobility, or the people exercised these three powers—that of making laws, that of executing public decisions, and that of judging the crimes and disputes of private persons.[7]

The American system has gone farther than any other democratic system in trying to keep the three functions separate, and to prevent the domination of any one. In order to achieve the latter purpose, it has allowed each organ of government to interfere with another in order to check its freedom of action. It would really be more accurate to describe it as a system, not of 'separation', but of 'balance' of powers. President, Senate and House of Representatives, for example, though all democratically elected, are chosen for fixed but different terms. They are 'separate' in the sense that members of the Administration are chosen by and are responsible to the President and cannot be members of the legislature, speak in either House[8] or even, (in theory) initiate legislation. They are interdependent because the President can override the legislature by vetoing a Bill, and because his veto can in turn be overridden by a two-thirds majority in both Houses. The President has the right to negotiate treaties, but these must be ratified by a two-thirds majority of the Senate. He makes policy, but is dependent on the good will of the legislature for the necessary legislation to implement it. The powers are also interdependent in the sense that the limitations on the powers of the legislature laid down in the Constitution are interpreted by a Supreme Court whose judgments are subject to no appeal. But it, too, can ultimately be overridden, if the

legislature agrees to amend the Constitution in order to legitimise what the Supreme Court has declared unconstitutional.[9]

If taken literally, such checks and balances could bring all
government to a halt. Their aim, however, as has been said,
was precisely to check the power of both government and
legislature in a federal system in which the constituent States
retained their independence over a wide field of political activities. It was a system designed for a federal State and has not
been directly copied by any unitary State, though some of
these have adopted certain of its provisions. It could not have
survived into an age characterised by intervention by the State
in almost all fields, without considerable modification. Federal
powers have been in fact both constitutionally and politically
strengthened at the expense of the States and, since the need
for cooperation and coordination has long since replaced the
need for checks and counterbalances, many of the rigidities
imposed by the constitutional text have been relaxed. This has
been made possible very largely owing to the growth of parties,
and to the building up of a vast system of extra-constitutional
negotiation and pressures behind the scenes, thus enabling
President and legislature to reach the degree of agreement
required by the Constitution. It is still possible, however, for
the American system to be seriously slowed down for considerable periods of time, owing to deadlocks between President
and legislature.

The parliamentary system has a radically different approach.
It is characterised by the close relationship between executive
and legislature, and by the requirement that the executive
must have the confidence of the majority of the legislature. In
the parliamentary system, too (though this is not an essential
condition),[10] the functions of Head of State and head of government are divided. Whether he is a constitutional monarch or
a republican president, the Head of State remains outside party
politics and carries out largely ceremonial functions.

At the beginning of this century, a French constitutional
lawyer, Léon Duguit, described the working of the parliamentary
system as follows:

> Political power belongs to two organs working in continuous
> cooperation and checking each other by the reciprocal action
> they exercise on each other: one is an elected, collective

organ, Parliament; the other a unitary organ, the government, embodied in a Head of the State. Parliament legislates with the help of the government, which help is expressed in the government's initiation of bills, participation in their discussion and ultimate promulgation, with a more or less extensive right of veto. The government carries on the general administration of the country with the help of Parliament, which help is expressed in a permanent and general control of governmental acts, intended to guarantee that the directing ideas which inspire the government's policy correspond with the opinions predominating in Parliament; and that control is made effective by the political responsibility of government to Parliament.[11]

Few Englishmen, and not all Frenchmen, would recognise this as an accurate picture of how parliamentary government functions today. The relationship between executive and legislature can in reality vary enormously. It can be one in which they are partners in the sense described by Léon Duguit, and this was in fact the kind of relationship that existed throughout the Third and Fourth French Republics. At its best such a partnership provided real cooperation. At its worst it produced conflict, because in a multi-party system in which the divisions within and between parties are such that both government and opposition are heterogeneous bodies, forming coalitions, often only on an *ad hoc* basis, the dividing line between government and opposition may not be clear-cut, and can, indeed, be different on different issues. At best, the cooperation is an uneasy relationship. At worst, it can become domination of the executive by the legislature. If that happens, the government can retain power only by modifying its policies in accordance with the will of the majority on specific issues, or by resorting to the dissolution of the legislature, in the hope that an election will provide a more stable majority. But, as has been said, the provisions for dissolution under the Third and Fourth Republics remained virtually a dead letter. Governments preferred to let the legislature have its way, if necessary, at the cost of repeated changes of government.

This type of parliamentary government, known as legislative rule (*gouvernement d'assemblée*) is neither more nor less democratic than the type known as Cabinet government, in which the cooperation between executive and legislature is one in which the Cabinet is the dominant partner, though the more positive rôle of the legislature is to many Frenchmen, for historical or temperamental reasons, preferable. There are those who prefer weak government, partly because, in a divided country with a multi-party system, government is thought of in terms of the interplay of reciprocal pressures rather than as a battle between two monolithic opponents. In such a situation, the weight of individual parties, whether inside or outside the government, is greater when the executive is weak, because parties can combine to destroy it or to threaten to do so, even if they cannot combine to replace it. It should be added that this *de facto* acceptance of, or preference for, weak government depends essentially on the existence of a stable economic system in which there is no obvious need for strong government, and also on the existence of an administrative machine able to keep both political and economic machinery ticking over while Ministers indulge in the luxury of government crises. It must be added, too, that there have been periods in France when this was not enough, and when government was rendered possible only by the willingness of the Assembly to grant a government special powers to legislate by decree over wide areas. That is a recipe that is neither recommendable nor necessarily exportable.

The British tradition has been one of strong government, because political divisions have rarely gone deep enough to prevent the formation of coherent government and opposition *blocs*. Strong government has been matched by strong opposition. The case for Cabinet government was already accepted by the middle of last century, when parties were less disciplined than they are today. John Stuart Mill put it as follows:

Instead of the function of governing, for which it is radically unfit, the proper office of a representative assembly is to watch and control the government; to throw the light of publicity on its acts; to compel a full exposition and justification of all of them which any one considers questionable; to censure them if found condemnable, and, if the men who compose the government abuse their trust, or fulfil it in a manner which conflicts with the deliberate sense of the nation, to expel them from office, and either expressly or virtually appoint their successors.[12]

This does not read like a description of British Cabinet government today, because Mill was not thinking in terms of the modern party system. Nowadays, it would need a serious split in a majority party for a government to be defeated in the House of Commons. Parties are defeated in elections, but their primary function between elections is that of supporting or opposing a government and, within the limits imposed by that obligation, of criticising and supervising the government along the lines described by Mill. Their main influence on policy is exercised within the party organisation, both inside and outside Parliament.

The British Cabinet system has gone farther than any other democratic system in achieving *de facto* control by the executive over the legislature. Parliament remains theoretically sovereign, and can dismiss a government whenever the majority desire to do so. In practice it does not do so (or at least has not done so since 1924) because, in a two-party system, governments are, except in times of war or national crisis, homogeneous and represent only the majority party, while the opposition is scarcely less homogeneous. Since the opposition represents the only conceivable alternative government, parliamentary sovereignty has become in practice party sovereignty. Bagehot's description a century ago of the characteristic of the British Cabinet system, as being 'the close union, the nearly complete fusion of the executive and the legislative powers'[13] was, perhaps, less true then than it is now, but the modern party system has made it true. The Prime Minister and his Cabinet have as much power as they can persuade their majority in Parliament to accept. And the increased dependence of representatives on parties has increased the government's powers of persuasion. The Prime Minister has as much power as he can persuade his Cabinet colleagues to accept. And their dependence on him has also increased. But this domination of the majority party in the House of Commons is possible only on condition that party cohesion remains intact or sufficiently so not to threaten the loss of a majority. The power of Parliament to assert itself is always there, even although, in normal circumstances, it is not exercised.[14]

Critics of this conception of parliamentary government feel that it has gone too far in the opposite direction from government by legislature, and that Cabinet government is in danger of becoming Cabinet autocracy. Some go farther and regard the rôle of the Prime Minister as becoming so dominant that Cabinet government is in danger of becoming Prime Ministerial government, or quasi-presidential government. Whereas, in the eighteenth century, the young American Republic was created in the fear that legislatures would become too powerful, in the mid-twentieth century, there is a growing fear that they may be becoming too weak to control adequately the vast discretionary power now wielded by democratic executives in modern industrial societies. Modern laws are increasingly becoming merely 'framework-laws', whose application has to be left in theory to Ministers and in practice to civil servants, who, thus, become subordinate legislators. Majority party and executive are bound together by their common party loyalty and by their common dependence on a party majority. In Parliament, the battle carried on between the two opposing sides is seen by some critics as being no longer anything but a façade, for the electorate has already decided which side has won it.

It is clear, then, that the term parliamentary democracy covers a wide range of executive-legislative relations. The two types described represent extremes, neither of which constitutes a picture that is consistently true, or necessarily permanent. There have been times when French governments have by no means been helpless pawns, and when British Members of Parliament have been far from 'rubber stamps'. The process is one of give and take, and the relations between executive and legislature at any given period in any given country can be determined by a whole complex of circumstances, in which personalities, party organisations, party strengths, economic and political problems and public attitudes all play their part. The essential requirement in a parliamentary democracy is that Parliament shall retain the power to dismiss governments. Whether it chooses or does not choose to use that power depends, to a great extent, on the nature of the fiduciary relationship between parties and their leaders, as well as on circumstances.

Not all parliamentary democracies accept the degree of party control that characterised the British system in the mid-sixties. Though General de Gaulle was able to bring about changes in the French system that brought it nearer to Cabinet government as the British understand it than it has ever been throughout the history of Republican government, the French, like almost all parliamentary systems, remains a multi-party system. Nor have the French opposition parties come any nearer to constituting a coherent opposition. In many ways, the French system under the Fifth Republic has been *sui generis*, and doubts have frequently been expressed as to whether the changes would be more than temporary. Since 1962, however, it has been a parliamentary system with a number of 'presidential' characteristics. The French President, like the President of the United States, is elected for a fixed period by the whole electorate. French Ministers are not allowed to combine Ministerial office with membership of the National Assembly. The system remains, nevertheless, parliamentary, because the government is responsible, not to the President (in spite of General de Gaulle's statements to the contrary[15]), but to the National Assembly which alone can constitutionally dismiss it.

Other countries, too—for instance, Holland and Norway—also prohibit Ministers from being members of the legislature, but they are far less 'separated' from it than are members of the Administration in the United States. In both countries, as in France, Ministers are allowed to be present and to speak in either House, whereas in Great Britain, they can speak only in the House of which they are members and in which they have a right to vote. These examples of less close relations between executive and legislature do not amount to separation of powers, but merely, as K. C. Wheare has suggested, to a desire to keep the government 'at arms length in the legislature.'[16]

It is clear, even from the few examples quoted, that the strength of parliamentary democracy lies, on the one hand in its diversity and its flexibility, and on the other in its concentration of political interest and controversy on the single arena of Parliament. At its best, the system provides in Parliament a permanent confrontation between a collective organ, the government, and a more or less coherent if not always collective organ, the opposition—a confrontation that seeks to inform the electorate and to present it with as clear a choice as possible between realistic alternatives. It provides a framework within which differing degrees of participation in political life are open to the citizen. Nothing, however, compels parties either inside or outside Parliament to be responsible, or to try to educate rather than indoctrinate the public, and so its very flexibility can make it vulnerable, if parties choose to indulge in competitive irresponsibility. In the federal systems, Australia and the United States, though one has a parliamentary system and the other not, the citizen has more than one political focus. He has local anchors in the form of State politics and State loyalties, and the field covered by State politics is much wider than the field of activity of local-government authorities in unitary States. But whether the system is unitary or federal, if it is parliamentary, both the levels of political dialogue and the stability or instability of governments depend on the nature of the party struggle.

The strength of the American system has been its combination of governmental stability, deriving from elections at fixed intervals, with a single national focus of interest centred on a President who combines the political function of a Prime Minister with the national, unifying function of a British monarch. To adapt Bagehot's familiar justification of the monarchy, the American President focuses the nation's attention, not on the Administration, which is not even a collective organ, but on one person 'doing interesting actions', whereas, in the parliamentary system, the government seems often to consist of a number of people 'all doing uninteresting actions'. That this 'personalisation' of power is attractive to the general public is clearly indicated, both by the increase in recent years of the publicity accorded to the Prime Minister, and also by the support in influential quarters on the moderate Left in France for a system which would combine government responsibility to the National Assembly with the institution of a President, elected by the whole nation, and heading the executive as well as carrying out the formal functions of Head of State. The aim of this proposal is clearly to have the best of both worlds—parliamentary democracy plus the 'personalisation' of leadership. It has yet to be proved that the combination of these two principles can be workable. Directly elected Presidents who are also Heads of State and heads of government are characteristics of the governmental systems of developing countries, though, in these, the one-party system has replaced parliamentary democracy, or has existed from the coming of independence.

In the United States, the Presidency has its weaknesses as well as its strengths. The physical and political strain of the double Presidential rôle is enormous. It can be catastrophic if the man does not measure up to the job. Since there must be some safeguards against the abuse of power in a democracy, the President's power to act is not, in practice, commensurate with the personal prestige and status that he enjoys as head of the vast political machine. The risk of inaction at moments of crisis, whether owing to conflict between President and legislature, or owing to the imminence of a Presidential election, can, therefore, cancel out some of the advantages of the personal focus on the President.

Judicial Independence and the Rule of Law

On Montesquieu's requirement of separation of the judiciary from both legislature and the executive, there is no basic difference of principle either among parliamentary democracies or between the parliamentary and the American system. All are agreed that the judiciary must be independent. There are, nevertheless, some practical difficulties in applying the principle that make it impossible to ensure one hundred per cent independence in practice. For instance, some person or somebody must be responsible for choosing judges, and choice inevitably involves the risk of political bias. The solution usually adopted has been the appointment of judges by the executive, on the basis of the advice of competent legal bodies, their irremovability once chosen, and the payment to them of salaries adequate enough to ensure their immunity from attempts to bribe them. It is not an ideal solution, but the only practicable alternative, that of popular election, has even more serious disadvantages. In the United States, the filling of some (though not of the most important) judicial posts by election has resulted in political pressures, as was only to be expected. The relations between electors and elected are essentially those of dependence, whenever the elected have to persuade their electors to re-elect them.

The real safeguards of judicial independence come from something deeper than anything that institutions can provide. They come from the building up over time of traditions of respect for the principle of judicial impartiality and for the rule of regular law, not only within the organs of government and courts of law, but also in the minds of the general public. No democratic system, as has been repeatedly emphasised, can claim to be able to decide what is right or what is wrong. And since the permanent absence of any unanimity on these questions is a basic assumption of democracy, the duty of all public authorities is to ensure respect for laws that represent the views of the majority at a given time. The first duty of the public is to use democratic machinery to see that laws do respect the views of that majority, and also respect the principles of democracy, which include the obligation to interfere with individual freedom only to the extent necessary to ensure that the will of the majority prevails.

The second duty of the public is to respect these laws. In no field of public affairs is the fiduciary basis of democracy more clearly apparent than in that of law enforcement. The whole system depends on the assumption that most people will, in actual fact, be law-abiding, because, if they are not, then the system must inevitably break down. To take just one example, it is possible for governments to secure the passage of laws making strikes illegal and imposing penalties including imprisonment on strikers. But no democratic system has either the personnel or the accommodation to imprison more than a few thousand strikers at a time.

Society, then, is itself responsible for determining the standard of justice. The judge's function is merely to provide an independent view as to whether the authorities have exceeded their legal rights of interference with the citizen's freedom, and as to whether the citizen has or has not disobeyed the law. In so far as his interpretation of the law is politically biassed, he can, of course, in the short run make the law, by making it say what it was not intended to say. The standard of independence of judges is, therefore, extremely important. But in the last resort, the majority must be, in a democracy, responsible through its representatives for what the law lays down, and for the ways in which the laws are interpreted.

Three-quarters of a century ago, A. V. Dicey described what, in his view, constituted the proper standards of behaviour in a democratic society, in order to ensure 'the rule of law'. His notions, in terms of precise political and legal procedures, would not be accepted as adequate today. But the principles that he laid down do still provide useful criteria by which to judge a democratic legal system. His first requirement was the absence of arbitrariness. The executive ought not to be free to interfere with the law, to apply it differently to different individuals, or to decide at its discretion to apply it at times and not at others. It is by virtue of this principle that police officers have to have warrants; that prisoners may not be held in custody at the discretion of the authorities, but only if they have been convicted in a regular court of law of a specific offence against a specific law; and that governments cannot decide without parliamentary authorisation that an emergency justifies them in suspending normal legal procedures. His second principle was equality before the law, by which he meant essentially that 'top people' should not be able to treat themselves, and should not be treated by the State, as being at any point outside or above the law. The traditional right of a British Peer to be tried by the House of Lords, for instance, did constitute an infringement of the principle of equality.[17] His third principle was that the recognition of personal rights ought to be accompanied by provisions for their enforcement. The essence of rights lay, he believed, not in declarations that they exist, such as those frequently made in constitutions, but in the extent to which the actual legal machinery ensures that they are respected and do not constitute merely pious platitudes.

In reality, as each generation discovers for itself, all such principles must be judged by the standards governing their application, and these must necessarily change as the relations between the State and the citizen change. Today, a great deal of State intervention is discretionary in the sense in which Dicey used the word. But the intention of the law in permitting officials to use their discretion is often precisely to avoid injustice—the injustice that can result, for instance, from making some kinds of legal provision applicable to all and sundry without taking into account special circumstances that might involve special hardship to some. The State intervenes too, to increase social liberties at the cost of curtailing private liberties, as for instance, those of property owners where their property is an obstacle to slum clearance or to road building. Today, it no longer seems adequate to provide all citizens with equal access to the courts, without providing them with the financial resources to avail themselves of the right. Every new liberty or opportunity for some is liable to create obstacles to the liberties and opportunities of others. Decisions as to what ought to be done must therefore be taken by those who represent the majority, but it is their duty to ensure that, within this framework, unnecessary hardship is avoided and unavoidable hardship compensated.

To this end, suitable institutions must be created to deal with grievances and supply redress where possible. Whether they are legal institutions, as Dicey assumed that they would be in the main, or whether they are partly judicial, partly administrative or political, does not really matter as long as their aim is to ensure the maintenance of standards of justice. Courts of law, administrative courts, administrative tribunals, parliamentary debates, public enquiries, officials such as the Ombudsman—all these are necessary, together with a vigilant public opinion that cares about justice. In this context, an essential rôle is necessarily played in democracies by those whose main function is not to support the Government, but to defend sectional interests or to exercise general supervision over government action, that is the organised forces of opposition parties and movements, both inside and outside the legislature.

9
Oppositions

The ultimate criterion of a democratic State is bound to be the
legal existence of an officially recognized opposition.

T. D. Weldon, States and Morals

The existence of political opposition – by individuals and groups,
by the press, and above all, by organized parties – is the litmus-
paper test of democracy.

Henry Mayo, An Introduction to Democratic Theory

Consensus has, or should have, little place in politics. American
Presidents (some more than others) feel it necessary to pretend
that consensus is both desirable and possible, because they have
no organized party on which they can rely to sustain them in the
day-to-day political conflict.

Henry Fairlie, The Life of Politics

Among democratic systems, as they have been defined in the
preceding pages, there is agreement on the need for an opposition, essentially because an election cannot be a choice, in any
real sense of the term, unless at least two positive possibilities
are open to electors. In Communist and other one-party systems,
the elector can exercise a negative choice by abstaining from
voting, but this is no more than a gesture. In such conditions,
elections are 'a race with one horse'.[1] If the choice is to be a real
one, the opposition needs to be well-organised, which leaves
room for discussion on the kind of opposition that is most effective, on what the functions of oppositions ought to be, and on
whether there ought to be one opposition or several.

The Functions of Opposition in Democracies

Whether the forces of opposition are grouped in one main
party or in several, the first essential requirement of a democratic

opposition is that it should be generally regarded as an integral part of the political system. There should be 'sufficient toleration of rival groups, with different attitudes, to allow one to foresee—if not with equanimity, at least without fundamental despair—their coming to power or otherwise influencing the governmental process.'[2] Without this 'toleration', or acceptance, there will not be 'the peaceful "play" of power—the adherence by the "outs" to decisions made by "ins" and the recognition by "ins" of the rights of the "outs"—'[3] that alone can make a stable democratic system possible. Opposition must be regarded as being no less legitimate than power.

The basis of opposition should, ideally, be a permanent party organisation, whose aim is to achieve power, whose principles and policies can be presented to the electorate as future government policies, and which can, therefore, carry on a permanent debate both within the legislature and within the country on how to complete the government's achievements and remedy its shortcomings. This is not to deny the utility of all other forms of political opposition, such as the press and pressure groups. But these are not directly aiming at power, at replacing the government. They are promoting sectional interests, and so are not subject to what more than anything else helps to keep the feet of both governments and oppositions on the ground—the need to carry out, or to be prepared to carry out, a national programme, in which the priorities of sectional interests have to be determined in the light of what the party in power believes to be in the national interest and within the national capacity.

There is no doubt that, if the inevitable differences between parties can be resolved sufficiently to allow of a single opposition platform capable of becoming a governmental programme, then the opposition becomes correspondingly more effective. To the extent to which different opposition parties have to concentrate their energies on outbidding each other for popular support, or to the extent that they decide to concentrate their energies on theories or programmes unrelated to the circumstances in which they might come to power, they are likely to prove ineffective. But political circumstances do not always permit of this degree of compromise and agreement between opposition formations. Some multi-party oppositions, notably in Scandinavia and Holland, have been effective over long periods. In British and American two-party systems, both parties have had their periods of weak and ineffective opposition. French opposition parties have been consistently unable to combine sufficiently to make the debate between government and opposition either positive or permanent enough for the electorate to be presented with clear alternatives.

Whether responsible or not, the opposition must always be at some disadvantage in relation to the government, because the stimulus to unity provided by the test of power is lacking, though this can sometimes be counter-balanced by the greater force of attraction of parties that are free to criticise or propose solutions to problems, without being obliged to pay attention to their consistency or practicability. In an ideal democracy, such policies ought not to pay dividends. In practice, they often do help to win elections, because the public has a short memory, and a mass electorate cannot be expected to be a competent judge either of the merits or of the practicability of policies, partly because it is characteristic of human nature to be more conscious of governmental failings than of governmental virtues, also because governments do, and oppositions do not, have at their disposal enough of the relevant facts to enable them to decide how far policies are politically and financially practicable.

Since power provides the best tools for the job, the best training for effective opposition is to have held power and to have reasonable prospects of holding it again. Long periods of uninterrupted power exercised by one party or coalition can, however, be deleterious to both sides. Without adequate stimulus from critics, governments can become slack and complacent, or even corrupt, but without reasonable hope of power, oppositions tend to become disunited or unrealistic, and so fail more and more to provide effective criticism. British commentators frequently suggested in 1964 that, after thirteen years of Conservative government, the Conservatives needed a period of opposition and Labour a period in power, in order to restore vitality and cohesion to their respective parties. Similar fears were expressed in the United States, after the long period of Democratic governments that preceded the election of President Eisenhower in 1952. And a commentator on the prospects of unity in the Gaullist party wrote in 1967 that 'one side [the Gaullists] can work together only if in power, and the other [the Left parties] can live together only if united by a common hostility to the government. If the present situation were to be reversed, general disintegration would be inevitable. The Left would be faced with the realities of power, while the opposition would be disoriented by its loss of power.'[4]

How Much Opposition?

The British view that 'The duty of an Opposition is to oppose'[5] does not, in itself, offer much guidance on the crucial question, which is: how much opposition is in general desirable? The practice of different democratic systems varies widely on this point. At one extreme, there is the Swiss system, in which there is no clear distinction between government and opposition. But Switzerland, though undoubtedly an authentic democracy, is an exception to all rules, owing to its history, size, geographical situation, long tradition of local independence and of direct democracy, and to the fact that some degree of direct democracy still exists both in the cantons and at the federal level. It is only natural that regular recourse to the referendum —that is, to the whole electorate over the heads of parties— should to some extent blur the boundaries between parties. At the other extreme, there are multi-party oppositions, particularly in France and Italy, whose only real link at times has been their common hostility to the government, but which are not organised to act as an opposition, because they dislike each other more than each of them dislikes the government. There are those who believe that the American system could not have survived unless Republicans and Democrats, whose basic disagreement defies precise analysis, had more often than not provided the country with a President and a Congressional majority of the same party—that is, with a government and an opposition. There are those who believe that there is in Great Britain today a danger of too much consensus, with the result that the ordinary citizen seems to care less and less which side obtains a majority.

In modern economic and social conditions, it seems probable that, if democracy is to survive at all (and this is by no means certain, as is suggested in the following chapter) then democratic parties will continue to move closer to each other. When, as already happens in both Britain and America, victorious and defeated parties often receive almost equal numbers of votes, it is obvious that the decisive sections of the populations must be thinking along not very dissimilar lines, represented by the centre elements of both parties. This development need not prevent the existence of effective opposition. It does not indicate that parties are becoming philosophically nearer to each other, but merely that they hold fairly similar views about what can and ought to be done between one election and the next— which is, after all, what elections are about. There is no need for the choice to be between black and white. It is only habit, and the fact that clear-cut differences make the tasks of party propagandists easier, that lead to hankerings on the 'conservative', or more extreme, wings of both parties for the return of the good old days when parties looked less alike, because governments had far more freedom of action than they usually have in contemporary circumstances.

The essential requirement for an effective opposition is to have enough cohesion both to defeat a government and to replace it. This is a condition that not all democratic systems can yet be guaranteed to fulfil. The West German Basic Law seeks to ensure that it shall be met by making it a constitutional requirement that governments can be obliged to resign only if defeated by a 'constructive vote of no confidence', which means that if the majority of members of the *Bundestag* wish to force a Chancellor out of office, they must at the same time elect a successor.

It is sometimes impossible to create an effective opposition when it includes parties on the extreme Right or the extreme Left, whose opposition is not merely to the government but also to the régime. What can opposition parties do, if their only hope of defeating a government is with the help of elements with which they cannot possibly combine to form a government? This is a problem that confronted the opposition in Weimar Germany, and that eventually led to the replacement of democratic government by Nazism. There were periods during the French Fourth Republic when governments were defeated by the combined votes of Gaullists and of a left-wing opposition in which the Communists were the strongest party. Both French and Italian opposition parties have been faced since the war, with the permanent problem of how much opposition between Communists and non-Communists is either possible or desirable.

There are really two distinct problems involved. The first is tactical, and related directly to the struggle for power. Should non-Communists refuse all coalition with Communists, pending convincing evidence that they are not working for the interests of the Soviet Union, rather than for those of the nation? Or is it possible to go half way to meet them, by accepting their votes, but without making any compromise on policy or having any intention of including Communists in a government coalition? Or is it possible for non-Communists to believe, or to persuade themselves, either that the Communist Party has now accepted the need for change by democratic methods in Western industrial democracies or, alternatively, that it is at present unable or unwilling to make a frontal attack on democratic institutions, and so presents no immediate danger?

All these arguments have been used at one time or another by one or other of the Socialist opposition parties in France, Germany and Italy. During the 1960s, the French Socialist Party tried, first to find a basis for cooperation without commitment, then for some specific agreement with the Communist Party, and ended by falling back on the apparent acceptance of opposition for a prolonged period without any prospect of Socialist-Communist agreement. The Italian Socialist Party, led by Pietro Nenni, first tried cooperation with the Communists in opposition, then fusion with the Social Democratic Party in the government, but finally the reunited party returned to the familiar position as part of a disunited opposition.

Experience of attempts at Socialist-Communist agreement has always shown that the first result is to increase disunity on the non-Communist Left, whose energies become concentrated on the effort to reach agreement in their own ranks on the desirability or otherwise of seeking a basis of agreement with the Communists, and then, if that question is settled, on the conditions on which an agreement is acceptable. The second result is to produce endless dissensions between Communists and Socialists on the terms of any proposed agreement. And the third, assuming that the efforts do not break down, is to restrict such terms to an electoral pact that merely papers over the cracks of disagreement, instead of offering the electors a positive policy.

In this situation, when a non-Communist opposition is dependent on Communist votes in order to have any chance of defeating a government, the only alternative to the above frustrating tactics is either to accept the prospect of a long period of opposition, together with the difficulties of having to fight on two fronts (against the government and the Communists), or else to seek some understanding with parties farther to the right, which will also be accompanied by problems and by risks of creating disunity in its own ranks.

The position of the German Socialist opposition was greatly simplified by the Federal Republic's solution of the second problem, which is an ethical one. How far ought the democratic principle of toleration to be applied to those who are themselves intolerant, and whose aim may be to destroy democracy itself? The German Basic Law, by making non-democratic parties unconstitutional, provided the German government with the necessary authority to ban the Communist Party. Neither France nor Italy has wanted to do that, and so, in the absence of such a readymade solution, have had to try to answer the question empirically.

No democracy can be expected to go out of its way to assist those whose aim is to destroy it, or to provide opportunities for violence which may have that consequence. But to suppress either small revolutionary movements, whether of Left or Right, or even large movements, as long as they are not actively resorting to violence, could harm democracy more than its opponents. They often thrive on opportunities for protest, but democracy can hardly be expected to thrive on practising intolerance while preaching toleration.

In this situation, all democracies face a dilemma. On the one hand, they cannot afford to tolerate intolerance to the point at which those who wish to practise tolerance are themselves prevented from doing so. On the other hand, to turn a blind eye to small extremist movements that may never get beyond the stage of talk, or that do not in any case constitute a serious threat, while taking action against larger ones that do threaten successful revolt—that is, movements that have more support than the smaller ones—is clearly a solution based on expediency rather than on principle. Moreover, it is unsatisfactory as a rule of conduct, because it can give no guidance on how to recognise the precise point at which the line has to be drawn between what is and is not to be tolerated. All that can be said is that it is somewhere between the point at which further toleration or permissiveness risks being a recipe for democratic suicide, and that at which lack of toleration unduly restricts the basic democratic right to oppose.

It is not surprising that democracies have drawn the line in different places. Some have been threatened by extremism more than others, and either fear it more or have less confidence in their own capacity to contain it or to recognise danger points. Great Britain has never had a serious Communist or Fascist problem. France has often had to meet threats from either Right or Left, and sometimes from the two at once. Yet, for reasons that have been discussed earlier, French opinion is traditionally less conscious than British of the dangers of extending democratic toleration to Communist organisations. The French Left fears above all being over-severe towards a large Communist organisation that thrives on martyrdom. The United States, which has never experienced any serious Communist or Fascist threat, is far more apprehensive about Communism than either Britain or France. Decisions have often been reached more or less by accident, or by purely empirical processes. For instance, from the beginning, representative assemblies of the various organisations for European integration included no Communists, though no concerted decision was taken on this point. Perhaps none was necessary owing to the hostility at that time of Communist parties in all countries to all forms of 'Europeanism'. Italy however, in 1969, decided to include Communists in her delegation to the Council of Europe and the European Parliament.

It would seem that, in general, the guiding principle on the problem of the toleration of intolerance has been a sense of obligation to impose only the minimum of restrictions on freedom of action compatible with the prevention of a major threat to the democratic way of life—to avoid, that is, all persecution and to recognise the rights of all types of movement to express their opinions, provided that they respect legality. To a very large extent, French and British Communist Parties have recognised their obligation to respect legality. On their side, governments have clearly hesitated as long as possible before taking repressive measures. It was only after flagrant and dangerous infringements of legality and prolonged violence that the extremist groups that provided the student leaders of the 'May revolution' in France were banned. They had been in existence for some time and had been not only preaching violence, but also practising it, though on a much smaller scale.

The question of how much opposition is desirable in principle, when there are no complicating factors such as an opposition divided against itself, is much easier to answer. Opposition for opposition's sake must, in the long run, diminish the quality of the democratic dialogue. The normal methods of party propaganda and debate inevitably produce some distortion of the facts, because it is the job of each side to present its own case in the most favourable light. The simplifications demanded by propaganda techniques and by parliamentary debating procedures produce something of the effect of Counsel for the Prosecution confronting Counsel for the Defence in a court of law. But whereas in a court of law the judge is there to guide the jury, the electorate—which is the jury in political life—has to sort out the merits of each case for itself, as best it can. To go beyond the point generally recognised to be admissible in a fair fight, and seek deliberately to mislead the electorate, risks discrediting the whole system by leading to an escalation of misrepresentation.

What is admissible and fair, however, is something that is decided in each country and in each party on the basis of habit, history and experience. It is also partly determined by the political climate and in turn helps to create the political climate. The limits of what is permissible will, in the last resort, be determined by the standards of conduct of the electorate itself. There are cases, for instance, where hecklers at a party meeting overstep the bounds and harm their own cause more than that of their opponents. However indefinable the boundaries may be, any political candidate becomes aware of their existence in the course of an election campaign. And in Great Britain at least, the speeches of almost any victorious or defeated candidate on election night specifically recognise that they exist by their insistence that the fight in their particular constituency was a fair one.

Opposition ought also to be constructive, if it is to teach the electorate how to choose between rival policies. In the normal course of events, government and opposition parties will have held power and hope to hold power, and so it is in the long-term interests of both sides to maintain a high standard of debate, and not to make unrealistic promises. Where an opposition is condemned to long periods without hope of power, there is nevertheless a steadily increasing temptation to indulge in irresponsible criticisms and promises.

Can One-Party Systems Be Halfway Houses?

The foregoing point of view is naturally rejected entirely by Communist parties everywhere. For them, any criticism must always be within the framework of a single legally-recognised party. Such criticism can constitute an opposition of a sort, though from the democratic point of view, it is only half an opposition at most. 'There is only one government that can be formed. There may be a choice of individuals, but there is no choice of party, no choice of government, no choice of policy.'[6] Soviet systems permit of no criticism, either inside the Soviet Union or outside in the neighbouring so-called independent States that make up the Soviet *bloc*, if it threatens to deviate too far from basic Soviet policies. The 1968 Soviet occupation of Czechoslovakia provided incontrovertible evidence of that. And, at the Polish Party Congress the following November, the Secretary-General of the Soviet Communist Party, Leonid Brezhnev, dotted the 'i's' and crossed the 't's', in a long speech which included the following warning:

... when internal and external forces that are hostile to socialism seek to reverse the development of any socialist country in the direction of restoring the capitalist system, when a threat to the cause of socialism in that country appears, and a threat to the security of the socialist community as a whole, that is no longer only a problem for the people of that country but also a common problem, a matter of concern for all socialist countries.

It goes without saying that such an action as military aid to a fraternal country to put an end to a threat to the socialist system is an extraordinary, an enforced step, which can be sparked off only by direct actions on the part of the enemies of socialism inside the country and beyond its frontiers—actions creating a threat to the common interests of the socialist camp.[7]

The meaning of the word 'fraternal', within this community could not be more plainly stated. The Soviet Union decides on behalf of all whether a threat exists and what is to be done about it. As for the partners, 'theirs not to reason why'. This is no more than to be expected from a system that claims to possess the truth. Divergences of opinion must logically constitute manifest errors, and be regarded as deliberate wrecking tactics, if opinions lead to action. It is only in democracies, which assume that nobody and no country can be sure of possessing the truth, that the expression of divergent views constitutes a basic right, and that systems of government provide for the regular exercise of the right by individuals, groups and parties.

Should non-Communist, one-party systems in the developing countries be classed in the same category as Communist systems? Most of them do not subscribe to Communist doctrine or want to join the Communist *bloc* (though they are often attracted to the Soviet Union, as being, in their view, socialist and anti-colonialist, as well as being a possible source of economic aid). It is less from conviction than from necessity that they are one-party States. As C. B. Macpherson has argued: 'The ideal of liberal democracy is consumers' sovereignty— we buy what we want with our votes. An underdeveloped country cannot afford this kind of consumers' sovereignty: it has too few political goods to offer.'[8] Or as President Sekou Touré of Guinea has argued more eloquently;

When the people's party, the party that really liberates men from all forms of exploitation, the party of the democratic revolution, has destroyed the bougeois or colonialist State, in order to build a State on the foundations of popular well-being, and on the political, economic, social and cultural development of all citizens without distinctions of race, religion, sex and social origins, it would be senseless to permit the formation of opposing parties representing the interest of sectional 'gangs'. It is not so much a one-party system, as a system of popular unity. As a popular and democratic party, the single party assumes the existence of a single language (which still has to be created), a single programme, whose principles and practice provide for free membership and for the expression of beliefs and philosophy—in a word, for material and non-material realities that form a single whole and so lead to one-ness. There is a world of difference between popular unity and Fascism, which rules by force, uses violence, and maintains itself through terror.[9]

Can it reasonably be claimed that these States constitute a special case, that, the road to Western-style democracy being barred to them, they are compelled by the facts of their situation to follow a different road, which may be the only possible road for them, whether or not it leads eventually to something nearer to Western conceptions of democracy? The thesis is an attractive one. Today, the title of democracy is effectively limited to the Western world—the European or English-speaking world, together with some of their former possessions. And, as Robert Dahl has pointed out, even there, democracy as defined in these pages is a very recent development. Of the 113 members of the United Nations in 1964, only 30 had an organised opposition.

Of the three milestones in the development of democratic institutions—the right to participate in governmental decisions by casting a vote, the right to be represented, and the right of an organised opposition to appeal for votes against the government in elections and in parliament—the last is, in a highly developed form, so wholly modern that there are people now living who were born before it had appeared in Europe.[10]

May it not be, then, that the developing countries have still not reached the second milestone, but that, once they cease to be in the position of trying to accomplish in a few years what it took older, stronger and richer nations a century and more to accomplish, they may feel able to admit the rights of opposition parties to exist? To some extent, this has happened. In Mexico and in Turkey since 1946, there have been opposition parties.[11] Ghana, which became independent in 1957 and a one-party State by constitutional amendment in 1964, recognised the right of an opposition party to contest the election of 1969.

Time, however, is something that can work both ways. It may take many of the developing countries a very long time indeed to develop stable political institutions. In the meantime, political habits will have been formed. It is difficult for parties and governments in power voluntarily to accept threats to that power. It is also difficult for oppositions, or potential oppositions, to maintain cohesion and strength when they are driven underground. They may find strength and cohesion in the unifying struggle for recognition, but this, in itself, like the unifying struggle for national liberation, does not constitute adequate preparation for the exercise of above-ground political responsibilities. Algeria found, after independence, that even the single dominant party that had led the fight for national liberation was totally incapable of carrying out the functions of a normal political party, and that the army was the only stable and organised force in the country.

The truth is that nothing provides the essential preparation for the successful working of democratic institutions except actual responsibility for trying to make them work. It would, therefore, be unrealistic to hope for more than a very slow and probably interrupted evolution of developing countries towards forms of government that provide for the regular interplay of parties, and towards standards of behaviour on the part of the electorate that demand the existence of more than one party. It may well be, too, that if and when the need for what has been called a democratic dialogue becomes generally felt, developing countries may evolve different formulae from those adopted by Western democracies.

The Dangers of 'Instant' Opposition

Nor are these formulae necessarily permanent. Developed democracies have their own problems, not the least of which is the growth in the 1960s of opposition movements that prefer to act directly and *outside* the machinery of political parties. There is no objection in principle to such direct action in democracies, provided it is ancillary to the opposition provided by organised political parties seeking power. Opposition expressed in the press, by pressure groups, by associations supporting various specific causes, by demonstrations—these and other forms of propaganda and protest are essentially such ancillaries, because they do not directly seek power. But there is a very real danger to democracy—as is discussed in the following chapter—in a proliferation of uncoordinated strikes and demonstrations (even though they may not resort to violence), if they come to be regarded, not as an ancillary but as a substitute for organised opposition as provided by political parties. The replacement of dialogue through regular and qualified representatives by direct pressures from demonstrators recruited more or less at random, or by direct pressures from sectional bodies that disregard the effect that the granting of their demands may have on the rights of others, constitutes a return to forms of action that are both primitive and anarchic. They do not permit of the coordination of sectional interests within the general framework of national interests, and they replace organised opposition by contradictory and often irresponsible protest.

It would be a sad epitaph on the long, often interrupted, and always difficult struggle for organised and civilised democratic government that began in ancient Greece, if it had to be summed up as a journey from *demos* to 'demo's'.

10

Has Democracy a Future?

I avow my faith in democracy, whatever course or view it may take with individuals and parties. They may make their mistakes, and they may profit from their mistakes. Democracy is now on trial as it never was before, and in these islands we must uphold it. . . .
Sir Winston Churchill, in the House of Commons, after the 1945
elections, 16 August 1945

Democracy necessarily involves some loss of immediate efficiency, but in the long run makes for its increase.
Clement Attlee, The Labour Party in Perspective
and 12 Years Later

Among the students and the young in West Berlin there is a vehement hatred of social democracy which is frightening. There is a similar tendency among the 'New Left' in Britain to regard social democracy as 'the main enemy'.
Peter Jenkins in The Guardian, 18 February 1969

. . . it may be that action is the only way to open fresh areas of consciousness. . . . The German living under Nazi rule could only exist as a member of the human race by blowing up everything in sight. Similarly, in U.S. society today, when all one's actions contribute at least in part to the wrong side, you may be forced into terrorism.
from an article by *Richard Hyland* in the Harvard Crimson,
October, 1969

Democracy in the 1960s

The most serious of all the problems that have beset democracies in the second half of the 1960s has been the growing disenchantment with both the idea and the practice of democratic government in the leading democratic countries themselves. There is no lack of diagnosticians of democracy's ills, and they provide a bewildering array of differing conclusions,

M

ranging from the explaining or explaining away of confusion or discontent as a by-product of industrial development and social affluence, to accusations of a fundamental disequilibrium calling for the overthrow of the whole democratic system. Citizens of Western democracies are criticised as being 'characterised by the psychological outlook of the spoiled child'[1], or as having a relationship with their governments that 'has become that of a consumer to a supermarket'.[2] They are pitied as convalescents unable to throw off the effects of two world wars, as apathetic or disillusioned, because their politicians disappoint them by reflecting too faithfully their own shortcomings as well as their virtues.[3] Those who condemn the whole system denigrate democratic leaders as bureaucratic and bourgeois capitalists, and their educators as élitist upholders of a class-ridden society. The only note of unison in this cacophony is the common recognition that there is something wrong with democracies.

This discovery ought not in itself to be either surprising or alarming, since modern democratic government is an experiment so recent in time and so limited in space that even the oldest and most successful systems make no claim to perfection or anything near it. What is alarming is the fact that a growing number of convinced believers in democracy seem to be pessimistic, or at least doubtful, regarding its chances of survival. Perhaps one explanation of the pessimism is that it is so much easier to see *what* is wrong (or is not yet right) than it is to see *how* it can be put right.

There is a fairly general recognition that political parties everywhere are failing to attract sufficient active support, and that their members are out of touch with opinion outside their own party, as well as at odds with each other within it. But is this development a cause or a consequence of the decline of democratic enthusiasm? And is it a sign of the general failure of parties to renew themselves or merely a manifestation of their lack of appeal to the younger generations? How do we decide what proportion of the population ought to be active party members? In a society in which all adults have the vote, a large number must be expected to be uninterested in politics. And the opting out of those who have neither interest in nor aptitude for politics may increase rather than detract from a party's efficiency.

What certainly does need explaining is why the facts of increasing abstention from participation in politics should coincide with the popularity of theories that 'participation' is a panacea for democracy's ills. If, as is often suggested, the moving force in democratic politics has been for most people the desire to obtain sectional and material benefits, rather than any profound belief in democratic principles, then it would seem natural that, in Western democracies, the rising standard of living should be accompanied by a falling-off of political enthusiasm. Fewer people will bother to fight when they have got so much of what they wanted. And the very fact that, in an affluent society, politics now have to compete with more obviously attractive pursuits could account for some increase in political apathy.

One consequence of the achievements of modern democracies has been the blurring of traditional party divisions, which, in itself, can discourage active participation in party politics. In the Europe of 1945, the political choices were clear-cut—public versus private control of major industries, planned versus free-enterprise economies, social versus private welfare. In 1969, whether party policies were concerned with social security, employment and productivity, incomes and prices, or with the Common Market or defence, the differences within parties were almost as great as those separating parties and even countries from each other. The issues themselves are becoming too technical and complex for all but a small minority to feel themselves vitally concerned, except where their own particular sectors and interests are involved. It is this development that, for many, explains more than anything else the loss of democratic enthusiasm.

> The crisis in democracy [said Isaiah Berlin recently] is fundamentally, I suppose, the difficulty of combining the political participation of a large mass of the majority of a given society in the processes which control our lives, with the inescapable need for highly trained experts and specialists for the purpose of controlling the very elaborate machinery which human ingenuity and genius has created.[4]

Sooner or later, then, discontent with the working of this elaborate machinery, together with the sense of remoteness created by the growing obsession of industries and governments with the problems of efficiency in relation to size, was bound to create problems for political parties, and so, eventually, for the democratic system itself. In the words of *The Times*:

A splendid discontent with the shabbiness of much of modern society can easily turn into contempt for the compromises which alone make a non-dictatorial society possible. A bafflement with the remote complexities of modern technological realities can easily turn into a desire to seek short cuts—embodied in the romantic image of a Che Guevara, the folk-hero of student ideologues, waging a perpetual guerilla war against society.[5]

The 'short cut' has been the response of an articulate and active minority among the younger generation. And the most obvious and spectacular result has been that, in the second half of the 1960s, the 'generation gap' has threatened to become a major element in the crisis of democracy. The problem goes far deeper than the traditional one of youth 'ginger' groups or rebel sections of political parties still dominated by older and staider elements. The unprecedented pace of industrial and technological change, together with the fact that the young of the 1960s have grown up in what is, socially as well as technologically, a different world from that of their elders, has transformed a gap into a gulf. The old cannot forget the past of unemployment, of economic hardship, of world wars and their aftermaths. The young have never known it, and some of them have no use for history anyway. Their international horizon is darkened not by the threat of the kind of wars that their fathers fought in, but of nuclear war. Their national horizon is one of full employment, social security, free education—all of which their fathers had to fight for—and these they take for granted without a thought as to where the money comes from to pay for it all. Their world is without the traditional anchors of established religion, sexual convention and class differentiation. They are, therefore, in one sense far freer than their fathers ever were—freer from want and the fear of it, freer from social convention. But too often, it is a purposeless freedom without any anchors to replace those formerly provided by the church, class conventions, economic necessity and traditional political allegiances.

What has really been a process of self-imposed alienation

of the younger generation began in Great Britain in the 1950s
with what were called the 'angry young men'. Politically speaking, it took the form of opting out of conventional party politics
and concentrating on world causes, such as anti-racialism and
nuclear disarmament. A British monthly review that devoted
a whole number to printing the views of under-25s on themselves in the late 1950s reported that the young found 'the
causes that bring men into the streets more vivid and real than
Fabian pamphlets and Tory dances'. The success of the Campaign for Nuclear Disarmament was regarded by some as being
essentially due to 'its rejection of all political affiliation and
political casuistry'.[6] The younger generation in continental Europe
tended rather to concentrate their interest either on advocating
the supranational organisation of Europe, or on various brands
of Marxist or neo-Marxist ideology. But whether the 'short cut'
was the championing of far-away and lost causes, or romantic
revolutionary or Utopian theorising, there was the same lack of
interest in, or rejection of, the traditional democratic party
structures and methods.

To the escapism of the 1950s, the 1960s added the sit-ins,
teach-ins, occupation of university premises, demonstrations,
slogans, banners, and also the violence, the deliberate destruction
of property and provocation of the police, that have been so
frequently associated with campaigns led by student radical
revolutionary movements in Europe, the United States and Japan.
These methods have not been used exclusively by students,
but it is only in universities and other institutions providing
for higher education that it is possible for so many young
people of the same age groups to be permanently available for
such activities. The special contribution of the student young
to the crisis of democracy has been made possible by the fact
that never before have democracies had so many students, so
many new universities, and so much serious overcrowding of
both new and old. Compact blocs consisting of thousands of
adolescents, artificially insulated for a few years from the normal
adult obligations of working for a living, with a high proportion
of individuals naturally attracted by theories, but often without the practical experience to recognise those that are spurious,
discontented in varying degrees, owing to consciousness of the
economic, intellectual, psychological or social problems created
by the rapid expansion of higher education and the changing

social climate—these have provided fertile intellectual ground for the spread of revolutionary theories, together with a permanent supply of physically manoeuverable crowds to support the demonstrations and protests that have become the everyday expressions of political feeling or economic grievance.

Crabbed Youth

But what are the protests about? The pretexts have varied from country to country and from one period to another. Some have been no more than the exploitation of the power of numbers in protest against genuine academic grievances related either to the organisation of higher education and its curricula, or to material conditions caused by overcrowding and by the difficulties experienced by universities in absorbing intellectually as well as physically the ever-increasing influx of students. In the present climate of disillusionment with traditional democratic methods, however, the exploitation of such grievances by militant student minorities has been used to mobilise the support of numbers of the younger and more naïve students for actions that are really intended by the leaders to form the spearhead of an attack on democracy itself. The militant leaders reject the democratic dialogue, preferring direct action. Tolerance of antipathetic viewpoints, which is essential to the working of democracy, is replaced by attempts by minorities to enforce their will *against* the majority, if necessary by illegal and violent methods. They replace the normal representative democratic procedures wherever possible by what is called 'democratic popular control from below', which means by decisions taken in mass assemblies and, therefore, liable to all the manipulation, incoherence and ineffectiveness characteristic of devices for direct government already discussed. They also create a world of contradictory make-believe, in which the democratic vocabulary is used in conjunction with openly admitted attempts to destroy democratic practices.[7] The admitted purpose of Daniel Cohn-Bendit and his supporters in 1968 was 'a series of revolutionary movements' (*des mouvements de rupture dans la cohésion du système*).[8] He himself believed that these revolutionary movements would fail, and leaders of militant student movements in Great Britain are no less frank on this point.

The student movement in Britain today [wrote one of them recently] will not ultimately succeed in achieving any substantial advances unless it wins its place within a revolutionary bloc much vaster than itself, under the hegemony of the working class. But it can meanwhile use its opportunities to act as a starting gun for wider social conflict.[9]

If they believe this, then their 'social conflict' is purely gratuitous. For in no country is there anything but hostility to them on the part of the organised working class. Indeed, their emphasis on the union of 'students and workers' is itself part of their make-believe world. In the words of the American undergraduate author of a book on the Harvard riots of 1969, 's.D.S. [Students for a Democratic Society] has a sincere but entirely theoretical commitment to the working-class because none of its members has the faintest idea of how the working class really lives.'[10] What, then, is their real purpose? To many of them, such a question is in itself a 'bourgeois' irrelevance. Their purpose is to find a purpose—to create a climate of violence, in which action will lead to the formulation of theory. As some of their leaders put it,

Revolutionary ideas will only be born from concrete engagement in mass struggle.[11]

A revolutionary culture is not for tomorrow. But a revolutionary practice within culture is possible and necessary today. The student struggle is its initial form.[12]

For the student generation of the 1960s it suddenly became clear that violence could have a liberating purpose.[13]

Democratic Fragility

It is evident that, worldwide though they may be, small, unrepresentative minorities of militant leftist students, who are materially dependent on the community for the resources that enable them to spend three years or more in universities and other institutions of higher education, could make no serious or lasting impact on strong and healthy democratic systems. How far their present aim to be a 'spearhead' of social conflict can constitute a real threat depends, therefore, on how far democratic systems can discover within themselves the intellectual and moral resources to recreate active faith in democratic government.

In the 1960s, three factors combined to give to such revolutionary movements an amount of attention and publicity out of all proportion to their numbers or to their real importance, and, at the same time, to weaken the resistance to them in democratic countries. The first is the ossification and apathy that has characterised an increasing number of the older generation. Whether their disenchantment with democratic practice is due to disorientation caused by the technological revolution, or to the fact that the spread of private affluence has led, not merely to the 'public squalor' deplored by J. K. Galbraith, but also to the growth of interest in private at the expense of public affairs, it has had important political consequences. A responsible Labour M.P. has recently gone as far as to diagnose a process of social disintegration in Great Britain that, in his view, goes far deeper than its 'uglier manifestations', such as football hooligans and skinheads. 'There is, today, [he said] a great big problem that just cannot be legislated out of existence in Westminster. It is the slow steady disintegration of the community itself. . . .' And this he saw primarily as being due to 'a rising tide of selfishness ... that drives all the socialising institutions—the schools, the hospitals, even the family itself—on the defensive.'[14]

This accusation has also been levelled at democratic communities other than the British. It can help to explain why the public's reaction to the student challenge in both Europe and America has been often so weak and hesitant. If it has any significant elements of truth in it, it also makes nonsense of the fashionable claims that 'participation' can provide a cure for the disease. For without superb organisation and enthusiasm, 'participation' becomes merely another series of 'remote' committees that will slow down still further a process of decision-making that it is urgent to speed up by democratic rather than by technocratic methods. Participation cannot be imposed. It needs willing and able participators, and it is precisely the lack of them at almost all stages of the governmental process that is one of the symptoms of the disease of political apathy.

The second factor is the changing focus of politics, together with the capacity of the mass media to distort the focus still more by its choice of news items, and to communicate speedily and dramatically (and sometimes inaccurately) to worldwide audiences, news and pictures of events highlighted in different countries. We are living in a world in which the scope for action by individuals, by nations, and indeed by international bodies, is continually narrowing, while, thanks to television, the horizon of individual interest in, and superficial acquaintance with, political events is continually widening. Vietnam and Biafra, demonstrations, strikes, violence—these, from Tokio to San Francisco, are nowadays far more real and immediate to most people than, say, decisions in either their local Council or their national parliament, not to speak of what happens in municipal or parliamentary committee-rooms, where the essential work of democracy is done. This is where 'participation' is needed, not in marches of protest against the Vietnam war about which the ordinary citizen can do nothing. There is no reason, of course, why such demonstrations should not take place if citizens want to hold them. But to the extent to which they choose the drama of ineffectual protest, the excitement of violence and of symbolic gestures, such as sitting on rugby fields or in Trafalgar Square in order to express feelings of anti-racialism, *to the exclusion* of the drudgery of everyday politics, they are joining the students' make-believe world.

As it is, it is too often student extremists who set the pace. This is partly due to the decline of democratic enthusiasm, but it is partly due to the third special factor that is characteristic of the society of the 1960s, which is not only the unprecedented increase in all countries, and especially in Europe and the United States, of the numbers of students, but also the current emphasis everywhere on the importance of youth. It is not merely that never before, in the history of democracies, have there been so many students, but that never before have there been so many arrogant and vociferously demanding young men and women, with time available to organise and participate in so many demonstrations, and the ability, therefore, to furnish almost any demonstration with the bulk of its participants, and with much of the violence that is becoming characteristic of political demonstrations everywhere.

In addition to these special factors, however, there are more deep-rooted causes tending to make democracies fragile. Because facts move faster than minds, and representatives tend to reflect the natural conservatism of the majority of their electors, democratic systems have a kind of built-in obsolescence. In theory, technocracies and totalitarian systems do not suffer from this handicap, because they are free to impose change and adventure, where democracies can only persuade (and where leadership is weak, often do not do that). In practice, they have their own handicaps, because, in totalitarian systems, representatives and agents tend to reflect the views of their masters, or what they believe to be acceptable to their masters, and so the bureaucratic and hierarchical rigidities of dictatorships and centralised bureaucracies can often make them far more out of touch with realities than any democracy.

The field in which the failure of the democratic dialogue has been most obvious in the 1960s has been that of industrial relations. This is understandable in a period of great industrial upheaval. When, to the innate conservatism of the average citizen in any country, there is added the conflict of sectional interests and the absence of any overall coordinating mechanisms for resolving such conflicts, the result is bound to be an initial resistance to change. This is a worldwide problem that no democracy has yet shown signs of being able to solve, though some of the smaller countries, and particularly in Scandinavia, seem to have been the most successful so far, perhaps because, as Rousseau saw, it is easier in a small country to promote consciousness of common interests. Whatever militant student organisations like to pretend, there is no significant body of 'workers' in any country—and the term 'workers' is used in its widest sense to include the whole working population—that is revolutionary, in the sense of being opposed to the present political framework of democratic society to the point of trying to overthrow it. Nor is there, in practice, whatever may be said in political meetings or published in election manifestoes, any revolt against the existence of the wage system. It is the way it works that is subject to criticism.

What has happened is that everywhere old machinery is being called on to try to solve new problems that it is not equipped to solve. The adaptations required in present-day economies are so vast that the conventional industrial organisations, geared to the negotiations of agreements between employers and employed, are totally inadequate. Governmental intervention in the interests of coordination and of ensuring the priority of national interests is everywhere becoming greater. The interdependence of different sections of the community is also increasing, and small groups of workers in key jobs can, by striking, impose hardship and discomfort on tens of thousands of their fellow-citizens, outside the bounds of their own industry. And as automation and other forms of modern technology progress, smaller numbers of individuals will be able to inconvenience larger and larger numbers of others. Yet industrial habits are still those of sectional rivalry and conflict, and their organisations reflect these conflicts. Governments and parliaments need the consent of citizens as producers no less than they need their consent as electors and members of political parties, but no democracy has as yet invented any machinery capable of obtaining it. Except in times of war, when there is a single overriding national interest, it is very hard for people to recognise and accept the sacrifices imposed by economic necessity, partly owing to the absence of such machinery, but also partly because the sacrifices often involve great disparities between one section of the community and another. It is understandable that, in the absence of any knowledge of the problems outside the field of their own immediate concern, some sections of workers should have taken a leaf out of the students' book and chosen direct action in the form of wildcat strikes, as the most paying 'short cut' to their own goals.

The resulting breakdowns of disciplined industrial dialogue, and the bitterness caused by the hardships imposed by continuing strikes have come to constitute a major challenge to democracy in the 1970s. The cost of failure to meet the challenge would not, however, be the realisation of the militant students' dream of 'an inner unity in the struggle of students and workers'[15], but a massive reaction of ordinary people from the perpetual annoyance and discomfort of strikes and demonstrations, and their attribution of failure to deal adequately with them, not merely to the government in power, as is normal in a democratic system, but, in the absence of evidence that any political party anywhere has the key to the solution of these problems, to the democratic system itself. The result could be the acceptance of some repressive régime (that might or might not be what students loosely call 'Fascist') as a price worth paying for the enforcement of law and order.

On a very small scale, that is what happened in France, both in 1958 and in 1968. In the first case, no government appeared able to bring the Algerian war to an end, and after four years, none could be counted on to secure the obedience of the army to the legal authorities. The majority of Frenchmen, therefore, accepted a Gaullist Fifth Republic, in the hope that a new régime, under new leadership, would be successful. In 1968, a majority moved to the Right in the general election, because the Left was associated in their minds with support for revolution and civil disorder.[16]

In both these cases, the reaction was one that remained within the democratic framework. There are those who believe that, if race riots and riots on the campus continue in America, the response will be a reaction that is both repressive and violent. If so, its first victims would be the revolutionaries themselves. The second victim could well be the democratic system, which is the only one that would allow militant students, strikers, and supporters of 'Black Power' the liberty that they now exercise as of right, including the liberty of trying to destroy the system and themselves along with it.

It has fairly often been pointed out that there is a striking similarity between the attitudes of American and European revolutionary Leftists and those of the Nazi movement. There is the same opposition to parliamentary institutions, the same intolerance that tries to enforce minority decisions against the will of the majority. There is the same cult of power, of violence and of youth.[17] The new Left may consider itself anti-Fascist, but it is not in spirit anti-totalitarian. It is in fact pseudo-totalitarian, because it does not understand the realities of power. The authentic totalitarians do, and it is they, not the new Left, who would be the beneficiaries of any breakdown of democratic society. It is precisely because the Communist party everywhere does understand the realities of power that it has, up to now, been one of the main bastions against any would-be union between revolutionary students and the organised workers.

Democratic Resilience

There is a sense in which all political systems are fragile, because human nature is fickle, and democracy could be regarded as being peculiarly fragile, because it is so difficult a system that it is a miracle that it could ever have worked at all. Its resilience has been in great part due to its being built on the recognition that human nature changes and on the effort to change with it. It is a fiduciary system seeking orderly change through dialogue, persuasion and consent. Some of its main difficulties have arisen from the difficulty of finding mechanisms enabling the necessary changes to be made at the right pace. There are times when the processes of democratic change are neither sensitive nor rapid enough to keep pace with the evolution of opinion, when the restiveness of critics comes up against the built-in Fabianism of democracy. The motto of the British Fabian Society, it will be remembered, is: 'For the right moment you must wait, but when you strike you must strike hard.'

If the right moment to strike passes unrecognised, then democracy can face a period of real danger, because its greatest vulnerability comes, not from the strength of the attack but from the weakness of the defence. It is the enemy within the gates who is most to be feared, the democrat who has lost faith in the democratic method.

Will the 1970s be a period of challenge or of danger? Is the following description of democracy's decline a pessimistic distortion, an imaginative prediction, or a likely epitaph?

> Today, parliamentarianism is in full decay. As soon as the form ceases to possess the attractiveness of a young ideal that will summon men to the barricades, unparliamentary methods of attaining an object without (or even in spite of) the ballot-box will make their appearance—such as money, economic pressure and, above all, the strike. Neither the megapolitan masses nor the strong individuals have any respect for this form without depth or past, and when the discovery is made that it is only a form, it has already become a mask and a shadow.[18]

This passage from Spengler's *Decline of the West*, published 1918-22, is a prediction that, up to now, has proved false. But the threat to democracy in the 1970s may prove more serious than any earlier ones have been.

The question is whether democratic defences can be mobilised in time to meet the threat, and the answer is likely to depend very largely on the courage and farsightedness of the ordinary parliamentary representative. Then, as now, it is Parliament that is on trial. Henri de Jouvenel once remarked, in a historic phrase, that there was more in common between two Deputies of whom one was a revolutionary and the other not, than there was between two revolutionaries of whom one was a Deputy and the other not. If that observation is still true, then there is hope for democracy. It is possible to restore to democratic systems everywhere the confidence and courage that they have seemed to lack in the 1960s. But that can be done only by the realisation that, whether they be conservative, liberal or socialist, politicians who believe in dialogue, who respect majority rule and the peaceful expression of conflicting opinions, and who want to maintain a fiduciary relationship in which rulers and ruled keep their 'covenants made', have more in common with each other, in spite of their political differences, than any of them have in common with those who are seeking to destroy these things.

The strength of democracy must be built on refusal to claim to possess the truth, and readiness to arbitrate between conflicting truths by democratic methods, and to the satisfaction of the greatest number. But it must also be willing to be subject to perpetual questioning and challenge. It will be as necessary in the 1970s as it was a century ago, to recognise, as John Stuart Mill did, that 'Democracy is not favourable to the reverential spirit.'[19]

References

CHAPTER I

1 Quoted in W. L. Davidson, *Political Thought: England. The Utilitarians from Bentham to J. S. Mill*, Williams & Norgate, 1919, p. 214

2 Reith Lectures, 1966–7, *The Listener*, 15 December, 1966, p. 882

3 UNESCO, *Democracy in a world of Tensions*, Paris, 1951, p. 527

4 Reginald Bassett, *The Essentials of Parliamentary Democracy*, Cass, 1964, p. 84

5 Everyman Edition, 1926, p. 217

6 Graeme Duncan and Steven Lukes, 'The New Democracy', *Political Studies*, June 1963, p. 161

7 R. A. Dahl, 'Hierarchy: Democracy and Bargaining in Politics and Economics', in *Political Behaviour, a Reader in Theory and Research*, Free Press of Glencoe, 1956, p. 87

8 Julius Gould and William L. Kolb, (ed.), *A Dictionary of the Social Sciences*, Tavistock, 1964, p. 187

9 Giovanni Sartori, *Democratic Theory*, Wayne State University Press, 1962, p. 3

10 H. Agar, *The Perils of Democracy*, Bodley Head, 1965, p. 68

CHAPTER 2

1 Funeral Oration of 431 B.C., Thucydides Book II, quoted in Leonard Woolf, *After the Deluge*, Pelican, 1931, p. 125

2 Ernest Barker, *Greek Political Theory*, University Paperbacks, Methuen, 1960, p. 21

3 Estimates of the number of slaves, freemen and resident aliens have varied greatly, and, indeed, probably did vary a good deal during the period of Athenian democracy. Ernest Barker in *Greek Political Theory* (p. 35) puts the number of slaves at about 80,000; resident aliens (or metics) at 90,000, of whom half were children; citizens, their wives and children at 160,000, of whom, perhaps 45,000 were citizens. These figures are estimates, relating to the fifth century B.C.

4 A. H. M. Jones, *Athenian Democracy*, Blackwell, 1964, p.12
5 *op. cit.*, p. 90
6 *op. cit.*, p. 44
7 *op. cit.*, p. 47
8 This comparison should not be carried too far. For instance, voting qualifications in the demes were not residential but depended on the citizen's hereditary right, and this continued to be exercised even if he was not resident in the deme
9 H. D. F. Kitto, *The Greeks*, Pelican, 1951, p. 129
10 Quoted in Jones, *op. cit.*, p. 48
11 *op. cit.*, p. 48
12 *op. cit.*, p. 48
13 Quoted in Plato's *Apology*

CHAPTER 3

1 *England's Lamentable Slaverie*, Tracts on Liberty in the Puritan Revolution, *1638-1647*, vol. III, p. 313
2 John Locke, *Second Treatise on Civil Government*, p. 149
3 Burke, *First Letter on a Regicide Peace*
4 Burke, *Speech at the Conclusion of the Poll*, in Works, vol. III, p. 19
5 Jean-Jacques Rousseau, *Social Contract*, Oxford Classics, 1947, pp. 372-3
6 *The Federalist*, no. 10, Everyman edition, p. 421
7 John Stuart Mill, *Representative Government*, Everyman edition, p. 280
8 *op. cit.*, p. 77
9 *op. cit.*, pp. 219-20
10 Viscount Bryce, *Modern Democracies*, vol. I, part i, ch. xi, p. 134

CHAPTER 4

1 K. B. Smellie, *A Hundred Years of English Government*, Duckworth, 1937, p. 14-5
2 *op. cit.*, vol. I, part i, ch. vii, p. 76
3 R. H. Tawney, *Equality*, Allen & Unwin, 1931, p. 289
4 Macaulay, *History of England*, chapter on the Toleration Act
5 D. W. Brogan, *Citizenship To-day*, University of N. Carolina Press, 1960, p. 13
6 *Liberals Look Ahead*, 1969
7 *Guardian*, 30 July, 1960
8 *Ibid.*, 3 July, 1960

9 Daniel Boorstin, *America and the Image of Europe*, Meridian Books, New York, 1960, p. 12

10 Bernard Crick, *The American Science of Politics*, Routledge, 1959, p. 99

11 The statement to the electors is reproduced in full in Jacques Kayser's *Les grandes batailles du Radicalisme, 1820-1901*, Annexe 3

12 Article 35 of Constitution of 24 June 1793. (*Les Constitutions et les principales lois politiques de la France depuis 1789*, par L. Duguit, H. Monnier, R. Bonnard, p. 65)

13 *Alain, Eléments d'une doctrine radicale*, p. 131

CHAPTER 5

1 Evan Durbin, *The Politics of Democratic Socialism*, Routledge, 1948, p. 235

2 For a comprehensive account of egalitarian and anarchist communities, see, among others, Charles Gide, *Communist and Co-operative Colonies*, Harrap, 1928

3 *Manifeste des Egaux*, in *Sylvain Maréchal*, Maurice Dommanget, Spartacus, René Lefeuvre, Paris 1950, p. 311

4 *op. cit.*, p. 311

5 Charles Gide, *op. cit.*, p. 152

6 *op. cit.*, p. 133

7 *op. cit.*, p. 138

8 *cit.*, S. T. Glass, *The Responsible Society*, Longmans, 1966 p. 69. See also G. D. H. Cole, *The Next Ten Years in British Social and Economic Policy*, p. 16, where he says the same thing even more frankly

9 see, for instance, *Industrial Democracy*, Working Party report, published by the Labour Party, 1967. A considerable amount of well-meaning verbiage does not succeed in obscuring the fact that these proposals do no more than provide for a better organization of contacts between management and workers, without changing in any way the essential nature of the relationship between them

10 Quoted in *Le Monde*, 12 July 1969

11 C. A. R. Crosland, *The Future of Socialism*, Cape, 1956, p. 73

12 Socialist Union, *Twentieth Century Socialism*, Penguin, 1956, pp. 15–6

13 *op. cit.*, pp. 26 and 29

14 Crosland, op. cit., p. 113

15 Young Fabian Pamphlet, No 7, *The Public Schools*, Howard Glenister, Richard Pryke, 1964, pp. 25 and 29

CHAPTER 6

1 An interesting and useful attempt has been made by Mr Leslie Wolff-Phillips in *Constitutions of Modern States*, Pall Mall Press, 1968, to identify and bring together the written constitutional enactments of the United Kingdom

2 K. C. Wheare, *Modern Constitutions*, Oxford University Press, 1951, p. 1

3 A similar vagueness characterizes the provisions of article 49 of the 1948 Italian Constitution which recognizes the right of all citizens to form parties in order to participate democratically in the formulation of national policies. Italy has the largest Communist party in the non-Communist world

4 The latter does so indirectly, by proclaiming in the introductory paragraph of the Preamble the attachment of the French people to "the Rights of Man and to the principles of national sovereignty as defined by the Declaration of 1789, confirmed and completed by the Preamble to the Constitution of 1946"

5 The following changes in the Constitution show the evolution of American thought in this field:

The House of Representatives shall be composed of members chosen every second year by the people of the several States and the electors in each State shall have the qualifications requisite for electors of the most numerous branch of the State Legislature. (Constitution, Article 1, Section 2).

In 1913 the seventeenth amendment provided for direct election of the Senate, the qualifications requisite for electors being the same for the two Houses.

In 1804 the twelfth amendment provided for the election of President and Vice-President by the people. The electoral college provided for under article 2 retained, however, the formal function of registering the popular choice, it being an unwritten convention that the votes of its members should be cast for the men chosen by the majority of the State electorate.

In 1964 the twenty-fourth amendment provided that the right of citizens to vote in any of the above elections 'shall not be denied or abridged by the United States or any State for reason of failure to pay any Poll Tax or other Tax.' This amendment does not, however, rule out the retention of the poll tax by States in State and local elections in order to restrict the right to vote

6 An example of this unwillingness to 'constitutionalize' a controversial issue is provided by the debate at the end of August 1946 on the thirteenth paragraph of the Preamble to the Constitution of 1946, dealing with education. The Communist spokesman, M. Jacques Duclos, admitted that he was not opposed to the recognition *de facto* of the right to teach in other than State schools (that is, that he was prepared to recognize the right of Catholic schools to exist) but he objected to this right being recognized in the Constitution by the inclusion of the phrase *'la liberté de l'enseignement'*, because this might make reform of the educational system more difficult. The paragraph, therefore, makes no reference at all to the rights of Catholic schools

7 *The Times*, 8 Dec. 1948

8 It by no means follows that every constitutional infringement brings such ideas into the forefront of politics. One instance can be quoted in which what most constitutional lawyers and politicians regarded as a flagrant infringement of the Constitution by General de Gaulle himself in 1962 ended up as a storm in a tea-cup, because it was no more than the adoption of an irregular short cut to a revision of the Constitution that the majority of political opinion was prepared to accept. On an earlier occasion, in 1961, General de Gaulle had to decide rapidly whether to stick to the letter of the Constitution – or rather to delay action until the constitutional position was clarified – and risk seeing the country involved in a civil war, or to commit what was possibly a technical irregularity and so safeguard future constitutional and political stability. The important factors in both these cases were, first, that opinion in the country was sufficiently in agreement with his political *ends* to condone some constitutional irregularity in the choice of the *means;* and, second, that most Frenchmen at that time regarded him rather than the Constitution as their main safeguard against political disorder and the threat of civil war. When, during the students' and workers' strikes of May, 1968, it looked for a brief period as if this was no longer true, then, for some political parties the revolutionary road began, once again, to appear as a conceivable method of getting rid of a government that they disliked. The difference was that, this time, the opposition parties were no longer in sympathy with what they regarded as General de Gaulle's political ends, and so some of them were prepared to contemplate, or at least not to condemn, the use of revolutionary means to achieve their own ends

CHAPTER 7

1 A. Phillips Griffiths, and Richard Wollheim, '*How Can One Person Represent Another?*' *Proceedings of the Aristotelian Society*, Supplementary vols. for 1968

2 J. Roland Pennock and John W. Chapman (eds.), *Representation;* J. Roland Pennock, *Political Representation: An Overview*, Atherton Press, New York, 1968, pp. 12–13

3 Hansard, vol. 440, July 1947, col. 284

4 J. Roland Pennock and John W. Chapman (eds.), *op. cit.*, p. 106

5 Harold Laski, *The Grammar of Politics*, Allen & Unwin, 1930, p. 315

6 On the weaknesses of the American system of primaries, see the letter to the Times (7 November 1969) by Keith Kyle, in which he makes the following criticism:

> The cost in time and money to the candidates for nomination would narrow the range of people from which candidates could be recruited (making it even more difficult than it is now for a person with legitimate Westminster ambitions to carry on a worthwhile career up to the moment of parliamentary election), and above all would make candidates who are not rich beholden to individual or institutional contributors who have chosen to back them personally rather than the party as such.
>
> Also, Conservative and Labour primaries would either tend to be fought on issues, highlighting the choice between the most distinctively Left-wing and the most distinctively Right-wing candidates, thus exaggerating divisions and disadvantaging the moderates; or alternatively would be contested between candidates undivided by issues, in which case the only possible subject-matter of the campaigns would be 'personalities', which would rapidly become odious. Examples of both types are found in every American primary season

7 Peter Campbell, *French Electoral Systems and Elections since 1789*, Faber, 1958, p. 45

8 Preface to Enid Lakeman and James D. Lambert, *Voting in Democracies*, Faber, 1960, p. 9

9 Maurice Duverger, *Les Partis politiques*, Librairie Armand Colin, Paris, 1951, p. 245–6

10 *op. cit.*, p. 247

11 Evidence in support of this is provided by the results of the 1964 election, when the Conservatives were defeated, after thirteen years in power. The 'unpopularity league' was headed by ten Conserva-

tive Ministers. See D. E. Butler, *The Electoral System in Britain since 1918*, Oxford, 1963, pp. 192–4

12 Peter J. G. Pulzer, *Political Representation and Elections*, Allen & Unwin, 1967, p. 55

13 Lakeman and Lambert, *op. cit.*, p. 149 and pp. 207–8

14 For a description of how these two systems work, see Lakeman and Lambert, *op. cit.*, ch. V and VI

15 Proportional representation has not had this effect in France, however, partly because a high proportion of Deputies and Senators are Mayors or Councillors for the *département* elected by towns or cantons within the constituency, and partly because the habits created by the two-ballot majority system have persisted through the comparatively brief periods during which proportional systems have been used

16 Sartori, *op. cit.*, p. 73

17 Letter to *The Times*, 22 May 1945

18 The Economist, 24 December 1966

19 Harold Laski: *op. cit.*, p. 322

20 C. F. Strong, *Modern Political Constitutions*, Sidgwick & Jackson, 1958, p. 288

21 H. D. Lasswell, *The Comparative Study of Elites*, Stanford, 1952, p. 7

CHAPTER 8

1 The term 'upper House' is used from time to time instead of 'Second Chamber', in order to avoid confusion, in view of the fact that both Holland and Sweden use the term 'First Chamber' for what others call Second, and vice versa

2 New Zealand became uni-cameral in 1950 and Denmark in 1954. Israel is also uni-cameral. Norway is basically uni-cameral in that its legislature is elected as one Chamber and then divides itself into two, by making one quarter of its members into a Second Chamber. In the federal systems of the United States and Australia, only the States of Nebraska and Queensland are uni-cameral

3 The consent of the upper House to legislation is constitutionally required in Australia, Canada, Holland, Belgium and Italy, as well as in the United States. In Sweden, the two Houses are not coordinate as far as the budget is concerned. Norway and Sweden constitute quite different special cases, which make it difficult to regard them as being truly bi-cameral. The two Chambers in Norway work very closely together and disagreements are resolved by a joint sitting. In Sweden, the government is responsible to the

two Houses jointly, although they are elected separately. As K. C. Wheare comments: 'In Norway, they have one chamber and pretend to have two, in Sweden they have two and pretend to have one' (*op. cit.*, p. 140)

4 France, Belgium, Sweden and Holland all have upper Houses chosen indirectly by representatives of local or regional councils. Another device, presumably intended to increase the prestige of the upper House is the requirement in a number of countries (France, Italy, Holland) of a higher minimum age for members of the upper House – presumably on the assumption that age brings wisdom. Though this assumption seems to be in process of being replaced in Western democracies by the opposite and equally false one that wisdom is a monopoly of youth, no country has as yet adapted its constitution to the newer nonsense

5 Address to Congress in 1861

6 The Swiss system is one of separation of powers in the sense that executive and legislature hold office for fixed periods of three years, and that if members of the legislature are chosen as members of the executive they are obliged to resign their seats. But members of the two legislative assemblies choose the executive, though they cannot get rid of it. The executive is not a party organ. Ministers can attend and speak in either House

7 *L'Ésprit des lois*, Book X, ch. VI. cf., the following passage from Blackstone's *Commentaries*: In all tyrannical governments . . . the right of making and enforcing the laws is vested in one and the same man, or the same body of men; and wheresoever these two powers are united together there can be no liberty

8 The President can, however, address Congress and deliver messages to it. His annual address on the State of the Union is delivered to Congress

9 This is in itself a difficult task, and is intended to be so, since the constitution represents the guarantee to the States on the basis of which they agreed to form a Federation. Amendment takes place in two stages. The first is the proposal of an amendment, which must be agreed on by a two-thirds majority in both Houses (or alternatively, by a Convention called for by the legislatures of two-thirds of the States – a procedure that has been used only once, in the case of amendment 21 repealing amendment 18 which introduced prohibition). The second stage requires ratification by three-quarters of the States (or alternatively, by Conventions in three-quarters of them)

10 French neo-presidentialist theories propose that a President elected by the nation should head the government and be responsible in the sense that President and legislature would face the electors at the same time, to eliminate the risk of conflict between them

11 *Revue politique et parlementaire* no. 74. Aug. 1900.
Le fonctionnement du régime parlementaire en France

12 *Representative Government,* p. 239

13 *op. cit.,* p. 65

14 In the House of Commons, the dividing line between government and opposition becomes less important at question time and when motions on the adjournment are taken. At these times, members of the majority party often criticise the government on matters of administration

15 See Press Conference of 31 January 1964, in which General de Gaulle claimed '*l'autorité indivisible de l'Etat, confiée tout entière au Président par le peuple qui l'a élu, qu'il n'en existe aucune autre, ni ministérielle, ni civile, ni militaire, ni judiciaire, qui ne soit conférée et maintenue par lui*'

16 See K. C. Wheare, *Legislatures,* p. 65

17 This privilege was abolished in 1948, after having fallen into disuse

CHAPTER 9

1 Mayo, *op. cit.,* p. 149

2 Bernard Williams, 'Democracy and Ideology', *Political Quarterly,* Oct. – Dec., 1961, p. 379

3 S. M. Lipset, 'Some Social Requisites of Democracy: Economic Development and Political Legitimacy, *American Political Science Review,* LIII, March 1959, p. 71

4 Dominique Bandes in *Le Monde,* 10–11 Dec., 1967

5 Quoted by Winston Churchill, in his life of Lord Randolph Churchill, as being a view expressed in 1830

6 Durbin, *op. cit.,* p. 239

7 *Soviet News,* 19 Nov. 1969, p. 66

8 *op. cit.,* p. 33

9 Sekou Touré, *L'Afrique et la révolution,* from extract quoted in *Le Monde,* 20 Feb. 1968

10 *Political Oppositions in Western Democracies,* Yale University Press, 1966, p. ix

11 Mexico was never a completely one-party State. Parties were given constitutional and legal status in 1946. The dominant party

continued, however, to win the overwhelming majority of the seats in the legislature, though somewhat fewer than before. In Turkey, the return to a multi-party system was followed in 1950 and 1954 by overwhelming victories for the opposition

CHAPTER 10

1 Sartori, *op. cit.*, p. 452
2 Henry Fairlie, *The Life of Politics*, Methuen, 1968, p. 244
3 D. B. Miller, *Politicians*, Inaugural lecture at the University of Leicester, 1958
4 Interview in *The Sunday Times*, 6 Nov. 1966
5 *The Times*, 2 June, 1968
6 *The Twentieth Century*
7 The following passage is typical: 'The revolutionary tradition of workers' councils has embodied this belief in democratic, popular control from below. The movement for 'student power' today is a natural descendant of this lineage. Resistance to it is resistance to the basic principle of democracy – the right of people to govern themselves. This right is only meaningful if it is exercised in the daily activity of each citizen in every place of work. The possibility of voting every five years cannot compensate for the absence of freedom in everyday life. The common demand for participatory democracy in its fullest and most explosive sense provides the possibility for an inner unity in the struggle of students and workers'. Gareth Stedman Jones, 'The Meaning of the Student Revolt' in *Student Power*, Penguin, 1969, p. 52
8 Interview quoted in *Le Monde*, 22 May 1968. *cf. Profile of André Manguy*, in *Evening Standard*, 31 May, 1968, by Peter Forster. In answer to a question as to whether history did not show that movements such as his produced effects that were the opposite of their ideals, Manguy is quoted as replying: '... that is perfectly true. Basically, I am utterly pessimistic about the result of what I am doing'
9 Gareth Stedman Jones, *op. cit.*, p. 54
10 Steve Kelman quoted in the *Evening Standard*, 5 Nov. 1969
11 Gareth Stedman Jones, *op. cit.*, p. 53
12 Robin Blackburn, 'A Brief Guide to Bourgeois Ideology', in *Student Power*, Penguin, 1969, p. 277
13 Gareth Stedman Jones, *op. cit.*, p. 38
Examples of the 'gratuitous act' are provided by

(i) the march to the Senate House of London University of 21 October, 1969. If this had any other purpose than that of making a fruitless gesture, that purpose was positively harmful to those on whose behalf it was ostensibly made. What purported to be a demonstration of solidarity against the victims of racialism in Rhodesia and South Africa, was in actual fact a specific demand for the cessation of the special relationship between London University and the multi-racial University College in Rhodesia which, even under the Smith régime, still had some 36% of African students. A condition of the relationship was that the College should remain multi-racial. The College students themselves were anxious for the relationship to continue. If the request had been granted, therefore, the result could only have been to make the position of African students even worse.

(ii) The Harvard riots of 1969. In the eye-witness account of this, published in *The Times* (Saturday Review) of 12 July 1969, and entitled 'Harvard on My Mind', Michael Holroyd reports that the demands that were the pretext for the riots could not be met because they were addressed to a body that had no responsibility in the matter, and one of them called for the abolition of a Harvard building plan that did not exist

14 Raymond Fletcher M.P., in *The Guardian*, 29 Sept. 1969

15 Gareth Stedman Jones, *op. cit.*, p. 52

16 See the description of the May 'revolution' by Alfred Grosser in *Le Monde*, 1–2 Sept. 1968:

'... *la révolution de mai, c'était le règne de la folie, belle ou non, de l'utopie, de la déraison.*'

The gulf between students and workers in France has been widened by the fact that the most militant of the anarcho-Syndicalists have been in universities whose students are largely recruited from the wealthiest parts of Paris, whom trade unionists (and especially the most important, Communist-led union) comprehensibly regard as play-acting amateurs to be kept at arms' length, except for limited purposes such as swelling the numbers of a Communist-sponsored march

17 Dr Tibor Szamuely in *The Swinton Journal* (organ of the Conservative College in Yorkshire) quoted in *The Times*, 12 March, 1969

18 pp. 519–20

19 *Representative Government*, p. 320

Notes on Further Reading

Giovanni Sartori, *Democratic Theory*, Wayne State University Press, 1962

M. Rejai, *Democracy – the Contemporary Theories*, Atherton Press, New York, 1967

Henry Mayo, *An Introduction to Democratic Theory*, Oxford University Press, 1960

Reginald Bassett, *The Essentials of Parliamentary Democracy*, 2nd ed., Cass, 1964

Malcolm Shaw, *Anglo-American Democracy*, Library of Political Studies, Routledge, 1968

David Thomson, *Democracy in France since 1870*, 4th ed., Oxford University Press, 1964

Equality, Cambridge University Press, Current Problems, No. 29, 1949

The Democratic Ideal in France and England, Cambridge University Press, Current Problems, 1940

Maurice Cranston, *Freedom, A New Analysis*, Longmans, 3rd ed., 1968

Leslie Wolff-Phillips, *Constitutions of Modern States* (Selected Texts), Pall Mall Press, 1968

K. C. Wheare, *Modern Constitutions*, OPUS 11, Oxford Paperbacks, University Series, 1968

Legislatures, OPUS 29, Oxford Paperbacks, University Series, 1968

Enid Lakeman and James D. Lambert, *Voting in Democracies*, Faber, 1955

Peter G. J. Pulzer, *Political Representation and Elections in Britain*, Allen & Unwin, Studies in Political Science, 1967

More Power to the People, Young Fabian Essays in Democracy in Britain, Longmans, 1968

Henry W. Ehrmann, *Democracy in a Changing Society*, Pall Mall Press, 1965

Index